Young + Brash + *Abstract*

January 18 – March 10, 2002

Anderson Gallery

Virginia Commonwealth University

School of the Arts

Richmond, Virginia

This catalogue was published in conjunction
with the exhibition *Young + Brash + Abstract*
Curated by John Yau
January 18 – March 10, 2002
Anderson Gallery
Virginia Commonwealth University, School of the Arts

The exhibition and publication have been made possible, in part, through the generous support of Virginia Commonwealth University's School of the Arts.

Works are courtesy of the artists.
Photographic reproductions of the artists' work are courtesy of Patricia Lyons with the exception of:
Walter Biggs reproductions courtesy of Thomas Powel Jr..
Theresa Chong reproductions courtesy of Danese Gallery.
David Brody reproductions courtesy of the artist.
Ana Vilarrasa reproductions courtesy of the artist.
Henry Brown's *Interlock* courtesy of the artist.

Panel discussion photographs by Jay Paul

Photographic reproduction of David Reed's work courtesy of the Virginia Museum of Fine Arts, Richmond. The NEA Fund for American Art. Photo: Katherine Wetzel.

Photographic reproduction of Jackson Pollock's work courtesy of the Virginia Museum of Fine Arts, Richmond. Gift of Mr. Arthur S. Brinkley, Jr. Photo: Ron Jennings.

Photographic reproduction of Nicholas Krushenick's work courtesy of the Virginia Museum of Fine Arts, Richmond. Gift of Sydney and Frances Lewis.

Publication Coordinator: Amy G. Moorefield
Designer: Laura Chessin
Editor: George Cruger
Text Coordinator: Shelagh Greenwood
Printer: Colormark, Richmond, Virginia

Published by the Anderson Gallery
Virginia Commonwealth University, School of the Arts
907 1/2 West Franklin Street, Richmond, VA 23284-2514
t. 804-828-1522 f. 804-828-8585
www.vcu.edu/artweb/gallery

Library of Congress Control Number: 2002101552

ISBN 0-935519-25-4

Distributed by the University of Washington Press
P.O. Box 50096
Seattle, WA 98145-5096

TABLE OF CONTENTS

Foreword by Ted Potter 3
Director, Anderson Gallery

Introduction by John Yau 5
Curator, Young + Brash + Abstract

Panel Discussion with John Yau and Four Artists 26
at Virginia Commonwealth University

Artists' Statements and Exhibition Plates 53

Artists' Selected Biographies 98

Exhibition Checklist 110

Ab-stract (*âb strâct´*): Considered apart from concrete existence. Not easily understood; abstruse. Affective content depends solely on intrinsic form.*

This book documents an exhibition of the abstract paintings of eleven young artists living and working in and around New York City. The exhibition was produced and presented by the Anderson Gallery of Virginia Commonwealth University's School of the Arts, Richmond, Virginia. Each of the eleven artists represented in the exhibit are engaged in creating works of art that are redefining the term ABSTRACTION. All eleven artists are painters.

In the fall of 2000, during a conversation with art critic, curator, and poet John Yau, I expressed my curiosity for what I was seeing as a renewed interest in abstraction on the part of younger artists living in New York and Brooklyn. What was beginning to emerge was not, however, merely a tip of the hat to the abstraction of their mothers and grandfathers. John had been thinking, for some time, about curating an exhibition dealing with the state of abstract painting in relation to a younger generation of artists working in the New York area. He was the perfect curator for this project. An experienced, intelligent, truly independent curator, beholden to no party line, or the marketplace. He's a poet.

Abstraction has always kept its secrets well, and has received its share of viewer hostility in return. It is not considered "good form" to go public and still maintain a veil of mystery, unintelligibility and enigma, which are abstract art's desired end.

In John Yau's excellent essay he speaks to the complexity and subtlety of the process of experiencing the art of the eleven young painters. Later in the catalogue, during a panel discussion, four of the artists speak about their work and their search for "community" in and around New York City.

The Anderson Gallery is part of Virginia Commonwealth University's School of the Arts. Important exhibitions such as this are encouraged by the enthusiasm and support of the School of the Arts' acclaimed teaching faculty, and by the leadership of Dr. Richard Toscan, our dean. It is rewarding to direct a university art museum within an environment of creative curiosity that welcomes such exhibition projects as *Young + Brash + Abstract*.

– Ted Potter,
Director, Anderson Gallery
Virginia Commonwealth University, School of the Arts

* The American Heritage Dictionary

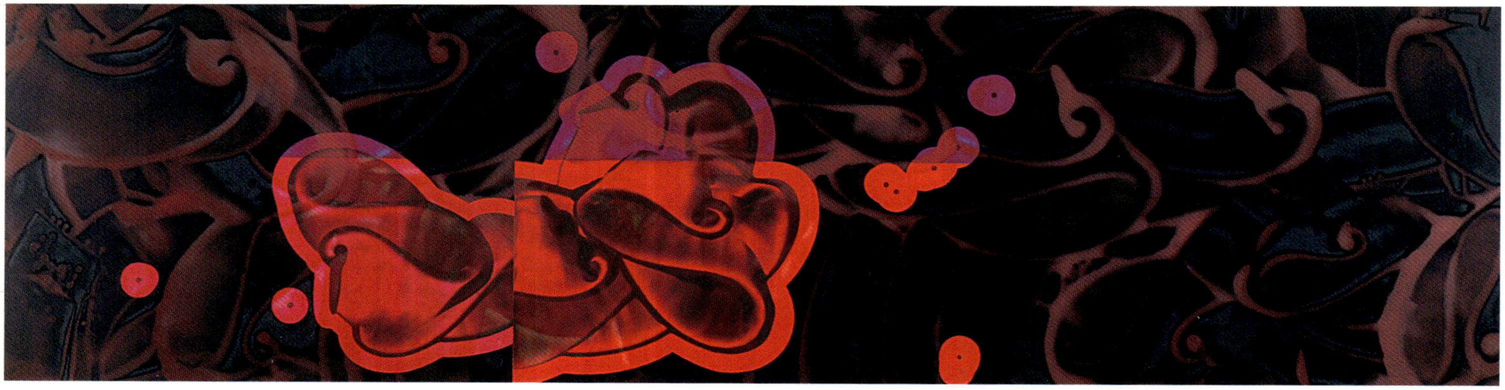

David Reed

#341: 1993, 1995, 1999

36" x 144"

From the collection of the

Virginia Museum of Fine Arts,

Richmond, VA

Young + Brash + *Abstract*

"There are two problems in painting. One is to find out what painting is and the other is to find out how to make a painting. The first is learning something and the second is making something."

—Frank Stella
The Pratt Lecture (1960)[1]

"Painting today lacks a shared rhetoric of purposes."

—Peter Schjeldahl
"The Next Pitch: Thomas Nozkowski and the Crisis (If there is a Crisis) in Abstract Painting (1996)"[2]

Introduction by John Yau

THE IDEA for this exhibition began germinating a few years ago, during a conversation I had with the painter David Reed. David is one of my touchstones, someone I go to with an idea, usually half-formed, about art. He never fails to help me gain clarity on whatever inchoate thoughts I have started obsessing over. Inevitably, he points out the patterns in the swirling bits and disconnected fragments my thinking has become. For in addition to being a great painter, David also happens to be one of the smartest, most insightful, and most thoughtful people I know. He knows lots of things and is very generous with his knowledge. Over the past fifteen-plus years, we have had long talks about Forrest Bess, Willard Midgette, Nicholas Krushenick, the Siennese painter Beccafumi, vampire movies, the TV show *Alias*, and baseball, just to mention a few of the subjects we have touched upon.

In this particular conversation, whatever I was initially thinking about evolved into a discussion with David about an exhibition based on an alternative history regarding Jackson Pollock's place in the history of art. Rather than continuing to recognize Pollock as a solitary hero whose poured paintings inadvertently announces both the culmination and demise of modernism and the hand-painted painting, he would be seen as a tragic figure

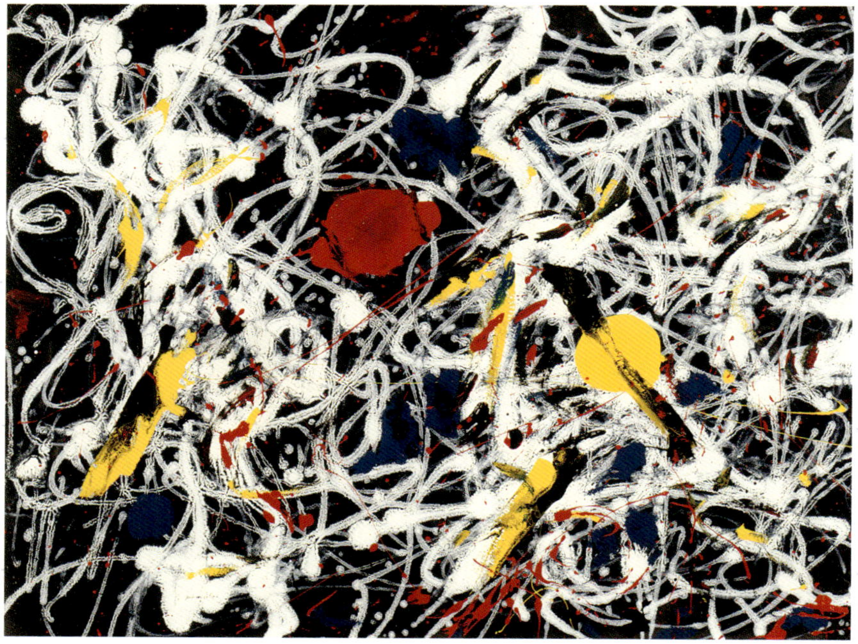

Jackson Pollock
Number 15, 1948
22 1/4" x 30 1/2"
From the collection of the Virginia Museum of Fine Arts, Richmond, VA

whose project was left incomplete at the time of his death. The focus of the exhibition would be on artists who believe the lines of inquiry taken up by Pollock did not end with his death, and that there remained (and remains) a whole range of unresolved issues. By mixing together the work of artists considered late modernist with the work of postmodernist painters, the exhibition would in effect counteract the segregating effects such terms have on the art world's thinking.

While the exhibition David and I talked about has yet to happen, I realized that once Pollock is no longer considered a figure of closure, then one must look at abstraction differently. For if one believes that Pollock's project remains essentially incomplete, then one doesn't have to defend abstraction. Sure, many people would continue to attack abstract art, and even look down upon it, but they can't help themselves. One just has to learn not to take every heckler seriously.

Some of the artists that David and I talked about were Norman Bluhm, Richmond Burton, Lydia Dona, Louise Fishman, Bill Jensen, Jonathan Lasker, Thomas Nozkowski, Brice Marden, James Siena, and Pat Steir. They were not necessarily the artists whose work would be included in the exhibition. It was that their work formed a starting point. What became more obvious during the conversation was that these artists share neither similar trajectories from Abstract Expressionism, nor the same sources and inspirations. And even when their work is informed by their close study of Asian art,[3] say, their paintings seem to have very little in common. And yet, while these and the other artists I have mentioned do not share, as Peter Schjeldahl observes, a "rhetoric of purposes," they are adamantly in agreement on one thing: abstract painting did not exhaust itself during the last decades of the 20th century. Perhaps, instead of lamenting the death of painting, we should start this century by celebrating both painting's vigorousness and variousness.

Chronologically speaking, the artists I have included in *Young + Brash + Abstract* came into their own around a decade after the generation that includes Burton, Dona, and Lasker began hitting their stride. For them, not only does Pollock's project remain essentially incomplete, but the projects of artists such as Agnes Martin and Robert Ryman must also be regarded as incomplete. They know that history is not what is found in books and magazines, but that it is what is happening in galleries and studios. It is, as Frank O'Hara observed, "the living situation"[4] that concerns them. Through their commitment to, as well as their belief in, abstract art, numerous artists after Pollock have successfully subverted the trope of closure. These younger artists continue that strong line of thinking.

Painting may be marginalized or adrift, but it simply isn't dead. I would further suggest that if painting and culture are inextricable, as they were in the Italian Renaissance, then being adrift is symptomatic of both the postmodern world and all the arts. Rather than continuing to praise quick solutions and irony, it may be time to honor dilemmas, opacity, and obdurateness. In a world that is continuing to speed up, it may be time to look more closely at artists whose obsessive works slow time down.

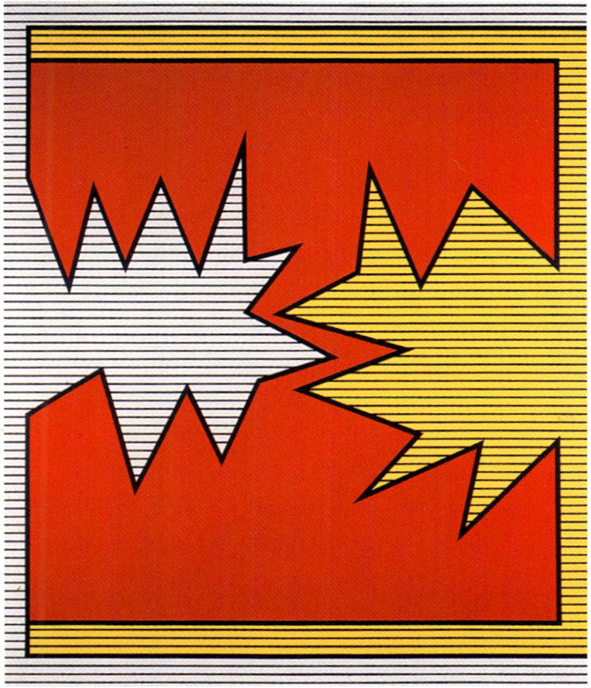

Nicholas Krushenick
Jungle Jim Lieberman, 1969
82" x 72"
From the collection of the Virginia Museum of Fine Arts, Richmond, VA

As far as I am concerned, when writing about Pollock, especially when he was championing him, Clement Greenberg did not go nearly far enough. He didn't follow through on the implications of what he observed was both true and groundbreaking about Pollock's work. For if, as Greenberg said of Pollock's poured compositions, they dispensed with a beginning, middle, and end, might that not also be true of abstraction itself? Who is to say where abstraction started, much less ended? Did it start in Peche-Merle, when one of our ancestors made a lasting mark on the wall? And was it Ad Reinhardt or Mike Bidlo who made the last abstract painting?

SOME GENERAL OBSERVATIONS

The artists in this exhibition do not constitute a group, and cannot be gathered under a rubric (Washington Color Field School or Neo-Geo). In this, they share something with the abstract artists who emerged after the heyday of Minimalism.

For while these younger artists share a number of things, it is equally likely that they disagree about lots of things as well. Even their definition of abstract art is not the same. Friction, we might remember, produces heat. And yet, the handful of affinities these artists provisionally share is telling, as much about them as about the state of abstract art in the first years of a new century.

Thus, the following observations can be made:

1] Many of the artists work with non-traditional materials.

2] Many of the artists have developed idiosyncratic approaches.

3] Many of the compositions emerge out of a dense accumulation of self-contained marks, lines, and bands. We tend to read these traces individually, as well as part of something larger. By composing this way, one which emphasizes a process that is both narrow and open-ended, the artists are able to stretch the viewer's attention between the smallest detail and the entire painting. There is no vantage point from which to see a painting. The viewer becomes hyperconscious when looking at many of these works.

4] Many of the compositions define or activate a space.

5] Many of the artists work on resistant surfaces such as metal, mylar, wood, or the wall.

6] In all of the works, the artists pay particular attention to the surface, and how to articulate space while underscoring the surface's tautness.

7] All the works exert a physical presence, though in ways that are significantly different from preceding generations of abstract artists. Thus the viewer encounters surfaces that range from a cold, machine-like luminosity to a lava-like topography.

8] Many of the artists do not limit themselves to working on two-dimensional surfaces. Thus, their entire body of work is not easily categorizable because they are just as likely to make objects that are neither paintings nor sculptures, but are hybrids.

9] There is a performative aspect to much of the work.

While the artists have many of these things in common, there are also extreme differences among them. Jennifer Riley paints wet into wet, Theresa Chong uses silkscreens to make her paintings, Kathleen Kucka tilts and turns the aluminum sheets to both control and direct her acrylic pours, Lisa Stefanelli has her aluminum surfaces spray painted before she paints on them, Hiroshi Tachibana scratches back through the final layers of paint, Walter Biggs introduces mica and graphite into his medium, and Chris Francione draws with a calking gun.

In some ways these artists can be regarded as the antithesis of Pollock. Instead of pouring looping, torquing skeins of paint, they accumulate small, self-sufficient details. In focusing on the smallest mark and each inch of the surface, they have seemingly turned Pollock's expansive outwardness into its opposite. And yet like a Pollock painting, their works pull us closer and closer. Rather than seeing these artists as reacting against Pollock, I believe they understood his work as embodying a grand permission, that it is an open field rife with possibilities.

In the very act of drifting, of intense disagreement about which way the nation should proceed, America seems to have unexpectedly provided these artists with an understanding that nothing is settled, that everything is up for grabs. One may become intensely and understandably gloomy about what the future might have in store, but that doesn't necessarily mean one must succumb to these unavoidable waves of despair. Painting is one of the few arts that has the power to resist all attempts to colonize it. Because we can't use up a really good painting, not to mention a great one, it becomes in effect our greatest natural resource. It can help us face a future in which the terms "less of" and "more of" will mean something very different than they do now.

THE ARTISTS

[Kathleen Kucka]

In her "Artist's Statement," Kathleen Kucka writes: "In this body of work, acrylic paint is my subject matter. I am working with the 'plasticness' of the paint. It can be sanded and poured, it can be cut and reattached. It's physical. There is sensuality in the paint's liquidity. It is a challenge to control."

By focusing on the medium of acrylic, as well as working on aluminum sheets, its resistant surface, Kucka arrives at something that is all her own. The number of pours are determined in advance by the composition or compositional effect the artist has in mind. The aluminum support functions as a smooth surface on which the paint dries. Another way she focuses our attention on acrylic's behavioral qualities is by limiting her palette to shades of white. The viewer sees a record of the paint's movement and whatever image arises when that movement is fixed. If Kucka isn't satisfied with the results, she can peel or sand off the paint. If she peels off the paint, she can choose to reattach it somewhere else. Gravity, control, and a resistant surface are central to the artist's pourings. In effect, she has redefined Pollock's pouring of enamel onto unsized canvas.

Pollock's enamel puddled on the canvas. It goes from encrusting the canvas, like lava, to staining it, like ink or dirty turpentine. In the minds of some, Pollock's pouring led directly to stain painting and the work of Helen Frankenthaler and Morris Louis. Kucka's work doesn't just challenge this reading; it subverts it by demonstrating that stain painting was not an ultimate destination, but a phase. I would further propose that the performative aspect of Kucka's paintings can be seen as extending out of early Brice Marden and Robert Ryman, the self-effacing processes they used to cover their surfaces with paint.

Kucka's paintings, their carefully controlled ribbons of paint, can evoke thick drapes and bridal dresses, domesticity and notions of the feminine, as well as aspects of science and seeing through a microscope.

Kucka draws by controlling the poured acrylic, directing it through her manipulation of the aluminum support. Whereas Pollock's swirling paint skeins are seen as emblematic of unbounded freedom, Kucka's controlled acrylic pours remind the viewer that all acts are finally bounded by both physical circumstance and time. Instead of denying gravity, as Pollock tried to do in his poured paintings, Kucka uses gravity to direct where the paint goes. In *Grip, Grab,* 2000, the acrylic forms striations like those one might find in wood grain.

Another contrast between Kucka and Pollock is in their respective evocations of space. Pollock's space is physical and layered, with the layers of paint pushing forward. Kucka's layered space is analogous to what happens when one looks at a seemingly flat surface through a microscope. Drawn in and towards, one encounters a textured space which hints at something more still to be seen. Looking becomes destabilized, becomes an act fraught with the knowledge that much remains hidden from view.

At the same time, Kucka's textured space invites multiple, and even contradictory readings. For in addition to evoking clothing and skin, to that which is revealed and that which is hidden or decorated, the paintings recall crystals, which are a combination of the geometric and organic. Eschewing the literal, which was the hallmark of many of the painters associated with Minimalism, Kucka shows us that paint can be both paint and something else, that its identity is not fixed, and that metaphor need not be avoided.

[Walter Biggs]

Initially, Walter Biggs's heavily reworked, otherworldly topographies seem to exist at the opposite end of the spectrum from Kathleen Kucka's paintings, their limited pours and the feeling that they are *premier coup* abstractions. And yet, I would also suggest that Biggs's tonal, largely monochromatic paintings can be said to extend out of Pollock's breakthroughs. On the level of appearance, for example, it's as if Pollock's lava-like encrustations kept growing and growing, until the paint became dense physical matter.

The surface of Biggs's paintings range from the delicately granular to thick encrustations. At times, they seem almost as if they could be both topographical reliefs of a distant, uninhabitable planet and specimens brought back to earth. Certainly, they seem to be a material that issued from nature as well as something that could only be the result of intense, hands-on labor. In making something that seems to be simultaneously fact and fiction, Biggs calls into question our whole orientation toward reality. As in Kucka's work, and the work of many other artists under discussion, looking is destabilized. Our sense of sight and tactility are fully engaged.

The sheer physicality and often shiny, constantly changing surfaces of Biggs's paintings pull us in, make us look closer at the way the painting interacts with the light. At the same time, the mineral-like surfaces are stand-offish; they offer no space in which the eye can take refuge. Looking becomes a visceral act; it makes one conscious of the gap between sight and touch.

Biggs's paintings, their dense materiality, evoke the world of industrial waste (slag, coal), as well as the natural world. They strike this viewer at least as the residue of a cataclysmic event, which could have been the result of either man-made or natural forces. By developing a palette made up of earth colors, and by being true to them as powder, dust, chips, grains, and flakes, Biggs reminds us that pigment is granular before it is suspended or dissolved in liquid. The drawing in these paintings is physical, the lines emerging as rivulet-like spaces and fissures cutting across the thick, uneven surfaces. One has the sense that the artist didn't apply the paint to the surface, but that the surface itself erupted. There is an unmistakable air of violence to these otherwise serene paintings.

Art historically speaking, Biggs's encrusted surfaces push Pollock's rough surfaces further, tilt them into the realm where the painting becomes an intensely tactile presence. At the same time, the tonalities are delicate, even elusive. Among the many paradoxes the paintings embody, one could consider the following. The paintings are both rough and delicate, seemingly a product of nature and something that is distinctly handmade.

In speaking about his paintings, Pollock declared, "I am nature." In Biggs's case, it is as if the painting itself made this declaration. Although heavily reworked, the surfaces are not painterly. Rather, they are self-effacing and, paradoxically, in-your-face. But paradox is not where Biggs stops, for his paintings impart a pleasure that goes beyond both the tactile and the visual, and engage one's capacity for speculation.

[Jennifer Riley]

Compositionally, Jennifer Riley's paintings tend to be divided into horizontal bands and lines of differing widths and physical thicknesses, with the lines often painted wet into wet. This way of working imbues the paint with a hint of liquidity; it suggests that something is becoming wet. The palette is tonal, the carefully mixed colors tending toward pale greenish-blues, grayish-violets, pinkish-reds, and orangish-yellows. By increasing the density of a color denoting adjacent bands or parallel lines, the artist is able to articulate a painted plane that is simultaneously tilting toward and away from the picture plane. Thus, illusionistic space is indicated through subtle shifts in color rather than through the more familiar device, perspective. Riley's articulation of space subverts any assumption the viewer might have that geometric abstraction is usually flat, with the only exceptions being a layered space.

Riley's control includes what happens when she moves a loaded brush across a wet surface. By introducing this aspect of paint's behavioral properties into a compositional vocabulary one associates with Agnes Martin, she shifts the serene bodilessness of Martin's paintings into a realm at once erotic and restrained. Riley underscores this erotic aspect of her work through her use of flesh tones, and shades of red and pink. Riley's combination of eroticism and restraint is provocative. After all, what is it that must be held in check? And why?

In another meaningful counterpoint to Agnes Martin, Riley's lines acknowledge gravity. It's as if their material weight has caused them to sag ever so slightly near the middle of a composition. The slightness of the sag suggests both fragility and strength, while, at the same time, evoking a body and hand moving through space.

In *New Rules for Romance*, 2000, the artist suspends a reddish line within a pinkish band. It's as if the lines are melting. The colors evoke flesh, as well as lipstick, the different shades they come in. In responding to the pink, the dissolving red suggests paradoxically that the pink is far warmer than one might expect. Meanwhile, juxtaposed against and within shades of greenish-blue, the heat of the red increases, and the play of opposites, of warm and cool colors, becomes a focal point for speculation. Through her combination of greens and blues, Riley arrives at a color that is appropriate to both sky and verdant landscape. Certainly these combinations, where one thing becomes another, are consistent with the states of revery one achieves during erotic moments.

By registering paint's liquidity in such a carefully controlled manner, as well as by acknowledging the unavoidable effect of gravity on the line, Riley transforms geometric abstraction into an erotic mode. Thus, another significant difference between Martin and Riley is in the metaphysics of their respective approach. In Martin, horizontality is associated with landscape, particularly the immense expanses of New Mexico, where she has lived for many years. In Riley's case, however, horizontality can be associated with the erotic body, the body both in control and on the point of losing control. By introducing this possible reading into the realm of geometric abstraction, Riley also comments on Martin's paintings.

In Martin's work, horizontality and luminosity can be read as evoking the point where the prone (or praying) body and the landscape merge and become light. By this I mean that Martin's horizontal lines not only evoke the horizon, they also evoke infinity, the immensity of a place that stretches out endlessly. Martin isn't, however, interested in the horizon so much as she is interested in the landscape above the horizon, the world of light and bodilessness. Riley's concerns are more earthly. The exalted states she embodies in her paintings are intimate and inward, if one understands that such moments can be both physical and luminous, inflected by gravity while denying it. The viewer senses that Riley's paintings are not about landscape, but about the landscape occupied by the erotic body.

In Martin's work, horizontality and luminosity can be read as evoking the point where the prone (or praying) body and the landscape merge and become light.

[Henry Brown]

Henry Brown both draws and paints in a single work. Because he doesn't remove the drawing or schematic plan from the painting, his work exists on two distinct yet interconnected levels. In each painting, he uses the schematic he has drawn to generate what will become the painted image. And yet, the connection between the schematic and the image never feels obvious or literal. There is nothing mechanistic about what happens after the drawing is complete. Obsessive and systemic, the drawing functions as a springboard; it enables Brown to make an imaginative, unexpected leap.

In Brown's paintings, the viewer sees the plotted pencil lines and the painted image, but the relationship between the two refuses to spell itself out. The viewer is left pondering the gap between the two. These gaps remind us that thinking is not linear, that a series of leaps and sudden insights can occur. The viewer is also faced with questions: When is something truly independent and when is something truly dependent? At one point does coexistence occur? Are these states fixed or are they always changing? Such questions make it apparent that Brown has introduced contingency into the realm of geometry. And in doing so, he has made the viewer aware that geometry itself is not necessarily a stable or a closed system, and its instability may enable it to gain a generative power.

As a tondo with a central, radiating, star-like, geometric image, *Interlock*, 2001, recalls stained-glass windows. At the same time, the flatly painted, diamond-like configurations surrounding the star-like image cause the picture plane to appear to be bending slightly, like a bubble. This illusionism destabilizes the painting by transforming what seems to be a flat, static image into something in a state of change. This aspect of Brown's work distinguishes him from previous generations of geometric artists. His geometry is animated; each state, including that defined by one of his paintings, is temporary. For example, *Reversal*, 2001, seems like it has just unfolded itself before our eyes.

The realization that there is nothing under the sun that is fixed is something Brown shares with the other artists I have thus far written about, Kathleen Kucka, Walter Biggs, and Jennifer Riley. Certainly, in sharing this understanding of reality, they define an open-ended mode of investigation. In undertaking an open-ended inquiry, Brown doesn't convey optimism so much as faith. He believes that painting and paint will take him somewhere. Process, rather than product, is what is important.

[Theresa Chong]

The surfaces of Theresa Chong's paintings are shiny and nearly perfectly flat, while the layering of different systems of abstract signs, gestural marks, words, and schematic images is crisp. The layered, airless space and overlapping systems are inviting, even mesmerizing, while the pristine surfaces are both alluring and aloof. For Chong, the painting is no longer a field or a plane. Rather, it is a color-saturated screen, which embodies an immeasurably deep space. Within this model for infinity, the systems of signs and the carefully inscribed images seem to be floating towards and away from each other, reconfiguring their relationship as if gravity is no longer a presiding force.

Chong's vocabulary is derived from grids which are comparable to computer circuits and complex diagrams, images that one associates with a computer's schematic graphics, freely drawn scrawls that suggest Asian calligraphy, and manic scribbling. In terms of her palette, her choice of colors seems equally wide in their references. One encounters colors that exude a tropical heat, others that seem industrial, and still others that remind one of an unfamiliar, dark wine or a 1950s kitchen. What binds all these different aspects and disparate elements together is the process of silkscreening.

Chong's use of silkscreen connects her to the pop artist Andy Warhol. However, while Warhol derived his images from mass media and popular culture, from what are the largely public surfaces of society, Chong gets many images from mass media's hidden spaces. Her diagram-like systems remind us that language is both overt and covert, that everything can be encoded to have a very different meaning, that X does not equal X.

At the same time, by accessing signs and images one associates with computers and surveillance systems, Chong exposes another aspect of popular culture; it is programmed to keep track of the individual, to register likes and dislikes so as to satisfy or defer those tastes. Thus, in contrast to Warhol, who was interested in second-hand experience, Chong focuses on the struggle to achieve individuality within a field of overlapping and competing systems, which range from computers to handwriting, and from the electronic to the handmade. Neither extreme, she seems to be telling us, is possible. One must constantly negotiate one's way through the collision of signs and competing systems.

Chong's juxtapositions, the sheer density of them, are at once harmonic and dissonant, qualities we might come to expect from a person trained as a cellist. Neither harmony nor dissonance are privileged in these dense, allover paintings. Rather, aspects of each inflect the other. The overlapping systems remind us that however much we may wish for it, living off the grid is not something that is easily accomplished. One is always inside many grids. And yet, as Chong's paintings make equally evident, the colliding together of different grids and systems results in unexpected apertures and combinations. Incommensurability is to be prized, as who knows what springs from it. Chong's vision is not of a closed world, but of one where the desire for order is ultimately predicated on the courting of chaos. Entropy is the only constant we inhabit.

[Steven Charles]

Information or visual overload would hardly describe Steven Charles's packed paintings. He drips and pours enamel onto his surfaces, and then uses the resulting sprawl of linear forms as a map to respond to, alter, and manipulate. Each painting is the result of many, many successive pours and drips, where the artist is always responding to the topography of stripes, splotches, clusters, and dots. After the initial pouring of paint, each time Charles pours or makes a splotch or dot, he leaves a trace of the previous layer visible.

Compositionally, the stripes can either be adjacent, as if bundled together, or they can meander, zigzag, and cut across other stripes and clusters. Charles's systemic methodology consists of moving from the largest to the smallest detail. He is continually refining his marks to a finer and finer minutiae, honing in or what he calls "targeting" the placement of the next drip, splotch, dot. From the largest curving tendril to the smallest, pinhead-size dot, every mark is calibrated. The phrase "fine tuning" takes on a new meaning when the viewer considers the amount of attention Charles has paid to each micro-inch of his often large canvases.

Charles's paintings are densely packed, mutating networks of lines, clusters, and dots. Among the numerous analogies that quickly leap to mind, one thinks of the wires packed into a telephone cable, overloaded circuitry, Fabergé's eggs, Australian aboriginal counting paintings spinning out of control, and the guts of a fantastical machine. The paintings evoke both macroscopic and microscopic realities. This often dizzying way of reading into Charles's paintings is consistent on every level of his work. The dots, for example, evoke both cells and soldering welds, nature and culture, while the entire painting can strike one as a satellite view of an overgrown, futuristic city. Is the city thriving or has nature started to reclaim it? Certainly in viewing Charles's paintings, one wants to stand as close as possible, as if wearing a jeweler's lens, to see the myriad details and interactions, as well as at a distance that is constantly being adjusted.

Whereas Pollock's paintings convey speed and expansiveness, Charles's paintings, their countless details, slow the viewer down. His intense, obsessive accumulation of details compels one to look more closely, to surrender to the physical, visual extravaganza of paint and color. This surrender parallels our experience of a Pollock painting. Unable to impose order on what we see, we begin looking for the different ways it manifests itself.

Among the numerous analogies that quickly leap to mind, one thinks of the wires packed into a telephone cable, overloaded circuitry, Fabergé's eggs, Australian aboriginal counting paintings spinning out of control, and the guts of a fantastical machine.

However, to Charles's credit, he is in no way derivative of Pollock. The jewel-like, encrusted surfaces of Charles's work have turned Pollock's expansiveness inside out, as well as made something new of it.

In their density, Charles's paintings echo the postmodern world, its constant waves of sensory input. We cannot possibly process all the information that washes over and through us. In Charles's paintings, we may not process it all at once, but we can return to it again and again. The information they embody can not be used up. This, of course, is the pleasure principle operating at its highest level.

At the same time, Charles's obsessive, complex patterning never becomes rigid or stultifying. An effect that is very nearly the opposite happens. Hallucinatory, recalling both psychedelic and psychotropic drugs and out-of-the-body states of seeing, Charles's paintings convey an ecstatic effect. They are about seeing in an exalted state.

[Hiroshi Tachibana]

In his "Artist's Statement," Hiroshi Tachibana recalls a terrible car accident he had when he was twenty-one. While he was unconscious, he had an experience of a space he remembers as being "immaterial, abstract, and imaginative." This space, he tells us, was bathed by a "colorful white light" in which every "single color" was also present.

Although Tachibana never explicitly states this, his memory seems to be, in modern parlance, consistent with descriptions of a "near death experience." However, I do not think the artist is avoiding this loaded term. Rather, I think he is trying to transpose a personal memory into paint, to suggest its experiential possibilities. He is trying to make the experience accessible, something that can be speculated upon by the viewer.

Believing that "space is everywhere," but is "subtle, hidden, and shy," Tachibana attempts to envision these spaces in his paintings. For him, the issue is how to make a potentially isolating human experience into something larger and more open, to go beyond the anecdotal. This dilemma is comparable to Jasper Johns remembering a dream in which he saw himself painting the American flag. Like Johns, Tachibana understands that he had no control over his experience. But, in recreating the perception in paint, he is betting that it can become telling.

Tachibana's layered paintings are done in oil and pencil. While the final layer of paint is whitish in tonality, the colors of the previous layers vary. At some point during his process, he scratches back into the paint at more or less evenly spaced intervals in order to reveal the colors beneath. The sense that something is hidden and waiting to be revealed is an integral aspect of the viewer's experience. Space is both layered and dimensional.

In *Monster of the Room*, 2001, the curving linear elements stretching across the middle of the painting convey an immense space. The space is evocative of both architecture (Roman Coliseum) and hyperspace. It is a space we feel we could enter and be embraced by. And yet, almost in contradiction to this space is our awareness of the painting's scratched surface, the colors poking through the tiny, delicate apertures where the artist has carefully removed small rectangles of paint. Surface and depth have been bound together by the artist's investigation of paint's materiality.

In *Monster of the Room*, the paradoxical space Tachibana develops is at once deep and tactile. Spatially, the composition recedes both visually and physically in ways that seem to contradict but not cancel each other out. For what is seen as deep space is also tactile and very much on the painting's surface. Rather than being disturbed by this contradiction, the viewer is apt to be soothed, such is Tachibana's mastery of the relationship between surface and depth.

By articulating a taut friction between the visual and the tactile, Tachibana maintains a remarkable, as well as provocative, consistency to the differing, contradictory levels (or depths) of space embodied in his painting. The tension between the visual and the tactile reminds us that one's experience of reality is not unified. Rather, in impinging upon one's different senses, reality reveals itself to be a network of dense, overlapping stimuli which one inhabits and tries to become cognizant of. Tachibana's search for a space both immense and intimate becomes emblematic of the dilemma facing both society and individual. What kind of spaces can we, and should we, create?

[Chris Francione]

The sources of Chris Francione's paintings come from a particular slice of popular culture, the stuff you might find in an adolescent boy's room. However, Francione doesn't replicate these images in paint; he is in that sense very different than the pop artists. Rather, he alters his sources, so that they are not instantly and reassuringly recognizable. It is this lack of reassurance that is a key aspect of Francione's paintings. For even when we finally do recognize the image, we are not necessarily comforted.

By replacing transparency and recognition with opacity and puzzlement, Francione adds a dimension of abstraction to his images. In this sense, he is far closer to the unjustly overlooked artist Nicholas Kruschenick than to the other pop artists. Kruschenick was the first abstract pop artist; and his work anticipates artists such as David Reed, Jonathan Lasker, and Thomas Nozkowski, as well as younger artists such as Francione.

At the same time, to both complicate matters and to further engage our attention, Francione uses a calk gun to draw his lines; they are stiff and tactile like hardened cake icing. Although we first read them as lines, they form an image that we do not recognize right away. In *Touchdown*, 2001, for example, the field of lines is an anamorphic representation of a football player scoring a touchdown. But before we can try and see this image, we become acutely conscious of the physicality of Francione's lines, the sense that everything has been stretched tightly across the painting's surface, like rubber bands. The tension between the physicality of Francione's surface and the stretched, distorted image they articulate is mind-bending. We keep shifting our attention from the echoing lines to the stretched image without being able to keep either in focus.

Francione's distortions of the body are also to be found in *Pink*, 2001, the source of which is an Anime image of two girls kissing. However, by removing certain details, the image becomes two heads melded together, thus a single pinkish, lumpish thing. The hair no longer reads as hair, but as vegetal; it hangs down like leaves. The possibility that they are leaves is underscored by the physicality of the lines; they are like the veins of leaves.

Francione's distortions aren't simply a reminder of what can be done with a computer or a camera. He recognizes that society's relationship to the body is undergoing rapid and ultimately unpredictable changes. These changes include the increasing use of prosthetics, science's growing mastery of cloning, and the development of cyborgs or surrogate humans.

Thus we can read *Touchdown* and *Pink* as the artist's response to a particular anxiety: What bearing will these changes have on paradigms of masculinity and femininity, male and female?

It is telling that Francione picked an image of a football player to stretch and an Anime image of two young girls kissing to erase. The former image is of a male succumbing to extreme pressure in order to score points while the latter image is of a world in which masculinity and the male are no longer necessary. Francione's distortions wittily underline what the figures are already making evident.

By stretching out the football player, Francione isn't calling attention to the plight of the contemporary male. He is reminding us that the male has always been willing to distort or alter his body in order to gain attention. And by erasing a few details, Francione isn't exacting some form of male revenge. Rather, he is both underscoring his own absence and further sealing the world the two girls inhabit. For while the tactility of the calk lines invites intimacy, the bipartite image recognizes only itself; it is both self-sufficient and self-contained.

We may believe we can affect the future, but we will not be part of it. The world Francione envisions is one where the self has undergone profound changes. And these changes are both exhilarating and disturbing.

[David Brody]

David Brody paints and draws with very different results. Although done in different mediums, the paintings and drawings do have one thing in common, a sense of place. As he states unapologetically in his "Artist's Statement," "I am looking for something concrete and habitable." However, by this he doesn't mean that he is trying to depict a recognizable landscape or place. He is not in this sense a representational artist. Rather, he is an abstract artist who does not deny paint's capacity to be representational. Brody arrives at this contradictory understanding of paint's behavioral properties by placing marks, strokes, curlicues, and blobs next to each other, seeing what option each of these small painterly decisions makes possible.

Brody's additive process can be said to be the opposite of Steven Charles, who hones in. Brody, in effect, does the opposite. He builds up a porous, layered field of small gestural marks, though, like Charles, in a manner that is unplanned and open-ended. In this sense, Brody is an abstract artist who works improvisationally within certain limits. He eschews expressionism, for example, and his marks tend to be straightforward, often running along a diagonal or vertical axis. This combi-

I am reminded of the visionary architect Bruno Taut's belief that the crystal was the perfect model for architecture because it encompassed both geometry and nature.

nation enables Brody to develop a spatial composition that is essentially geometric.

Brody's paintings maintain a palpable tension between an accumulation of abstract, non-descriptive marks of paint and what appears to be a structural conglomeration. The sense of place is underscored by the paintings's titles. Each is titled *Region* and numbered sequentially. Brody's "regions" seem to be the result of a collision between nature and culture, the organic and the manmade.

I am reminded of the visionary architect Bruno Taut's belief that the crystal was the perfect model for architecture because it encompassed both geometry and nature. It is also worth remembering that Taut wrote science fiction in addition to theorizing about architecture. Certainly, Brody's paintings invite comparison to science-fiction landscapes and cityscapes, as well as to Chinese landscape painting, weird mountain formations, and organic structures in a state of change. And yet Brody's real subject is finally paint itself.

With a Brody painting, the viewer never forgets that it is a surface covered with paint. It's as if the image is struggling to emerge from the accumulations of paint, even as it is being subsumed by the tactile marks and strokes. The parallel strokes of paint crisscrossing each other convey a network of interconnected structures and modules. Brody underscores the modular aspect of his work by working on square formats which he can join together to make vertical or horizontal formats. For all their evocation of architecture, the paintings can also be understood in terms of music. It's as if Brody works contrapuntally, with each mark or series of marks responding to what went before. The result isn't a narrative, but an abstract structure.

In his drawings, Brody makes diagonal and vertical lines on the wall. The underlying grid is isometric. By using an isometric grid, Brody is able to articulate a dynamic spatiality made up of diagonal planes. As in his paintings, Brody delimits what he can both do and use in a drawing. In this sense, he is classical in his approach to painting and drawing. And yet his work isn't nostalgic; it doesn't look back with longing. His structures may be inhabitable by the viewer's eye, but that doesn't mean they are completely comforting. In Brody's paintings and drawings, utopian and dystopian impulses have become, as perhaps they always were, inseparable.

[Ana Vilarrasa]

Ana Vilarrasa's paintings are essentially square planes which round into a curve. The curved side faces the wall, while the flat side faces the viewer. They are both paintings and sculptural objects, uncategorizable hybrids. The palette is usually restricted to two colors. Thus, the flat plane is one color, except along the edges or at the four corners, where another color is used. The curving back may be a different color or the same.

In these works, one senses that Vilarrasa is trying to discover all the permutations possible within her rigorously delimited vocabulary. By limiting her palette, Vilarrasa establishes a dialogue between the front and back of her painting. We must recognize it as a self-contained object, even though we cannot see it in its entirety.

Both as hybrid object and as monochromatic surface, Vilarrasa's paintings are part of the family that includes the work of Robert Ryman. Like Ryman, Vilarrasa underscores painting as a flat thing, an object where all the visible sides must be attended to. In Vilarrasa's case, she has gone one step further. The back is part of the front and vice versa. They cannot be separated. Thus, by limiting her palette, the artist is able to make the viewer hyperconscious that a painting is more than a surface, that is a physical presence, an object.

In a number of her paintings, the source is a work she saw in a museum. Rather than copying the source or making an ironic comment on it, Vilarrasa uses a limited palette to interpret it. The colors may or may not be derived from the source; in each case, the decisions are made for different reasons. Thus, while Vilarrasa's paintings share something with her Minimalist forebears, they are different in that the artist embraces the past, and tries to make use of it. In this regard, she is closer to Brice Marden, say, than to Robert Ryman.

Because she both suspends the narrative and jettisons the pictorial aspect, Vilarrasa largely relies on color to bring her closer to her sources. Her slightly modulated, monochromatic planes aren't Minimalist paintings so much as emotionally loaded objects. She may be ridding her work of all the stories one associates with the spiritual, but she isn't being anti-spiritual. Just the opposite, in fact. One senses that these paintings, so precarious in their relationship to the wall, can be understood as surrogate bodies, as metaphors for the suffering that is an inherent part of living. And yet, the serenity these paintings exude conveys a kind of unmistakable secular grace.

[Lisa Stefanelli]

In her "Artist's Statement," Stefanelli states that she "spent the better part of [her] formative years training for national competition as a figure skater." While one can read Stefanelli's complex arabesques of paint as having their source in her experience as a figure skater, I think one must also understood her paintings in a context that goes far beyond the strictly autobiographical. Stefanelli doesn't transpose her memories of being a figure skater into painting; her work is neither anecdotal nor representational. Certainly, her arabesques evoke a far wider range of sources than her experience as a figure skater. Among other things, they recall the *Book of Kells*, Art Nouveau's lush forms, Persian calligraphy, William Blake's synthesis of art and poetry, hot rod pinstriping, and Pollock's torquing skeins of paint.

For one thing, she has combined geometry and gesture into a vocabulary of unpredictable, complex, eye-catching arabesques, the execution of which strike this viewer at least as both flawless and unimpeded.

The tracings of the blades on ice, and the perfect geometry Stefanelli was capable of making by moving through space, have given her a unique perspective on abstract art. For one thing, she has combined geometry and gesture into a vocabulary of unpredictable, complex, eye-catching arabesques, the execution of which strike this viewer at least as both flawless and unimpeded. The mastery seems natural, inborn. Of course, nothing could be further from the truth. Stefanelli simply isn't interested in showing us the struggle. For to do so would be to ask for the viewer's sympathy, which is surely a way to distract one from actually focusing on the painting itself.

Swelling and thinning, Stefanelli's incredibly sinuous line can be read as an inscription; it cuts and animates the surface, transforms it into a space. The sinuousness gives the line a dynamic presence; it is not only describing itself, but is also conveying a dance-like movement through space. One can see these paintings both as figural presences and as records of a figure's movements both through space and across a surface. At the same time, the lines evoke Gothic tales in which everything is capable of being animated by demonic forces. Can we not read her lines as tree roots coming to life? Can we not read her reds as a sign of a life force coming to life? Thus, the lines feel both man-made and organic.

Stefanelli's line can be read as both paint and a highly elaborated picture of paint's liquidity. Thus, it has affinities to the paintings of David Reed and Norman Bluhm. Although ostensibly flat, Stefanelli's subtle shifts in color animate the line, transform it into physical though largely flat form, a silhouette. We cannot tell if we are seeing the silhouette in profile or if it is facing us.

Stefanelli's compositions range from complex symmetries to an asymmetrical network of whiplashing curves, twists, and turns. By turns calligraphic, gestural, and decorative, Stefanelli has extended Pollock's arabesques in an unexpected direction. Her paintings are both elegant and idiosyncratic, both matter-of-fact and richly metaphorical. In this regard, Stefanelli's work shares something with the other work in the show. Taken together, these artists and their work, the different paths they have taken, are further proof of the healthy state of both abstraction and painting today.

[NOTES]

1 Frank Stella: *The Black Paintings* (Baltimore: Baltimore Museum of Art, 1976), p. 78.

2 Thomas Nozkowski: *10 Paintings* (Washington DC; Baumgartner Galleries, 1996), p. 4.

3 *Looking East: Brice Marden, Michael Mazur, Pat Steir* (Seattle and London: University of Washington Press and Boston University Art Gallery, 2002). Both the exhibition and the accompanying catalog essays suggest that there is more than one reading regarding the incompleteness of Pollock's project.

4 Art Chronicles 1954-1966, *Frank O'Hara* (New York: George Braziller, 1975), p. 5.

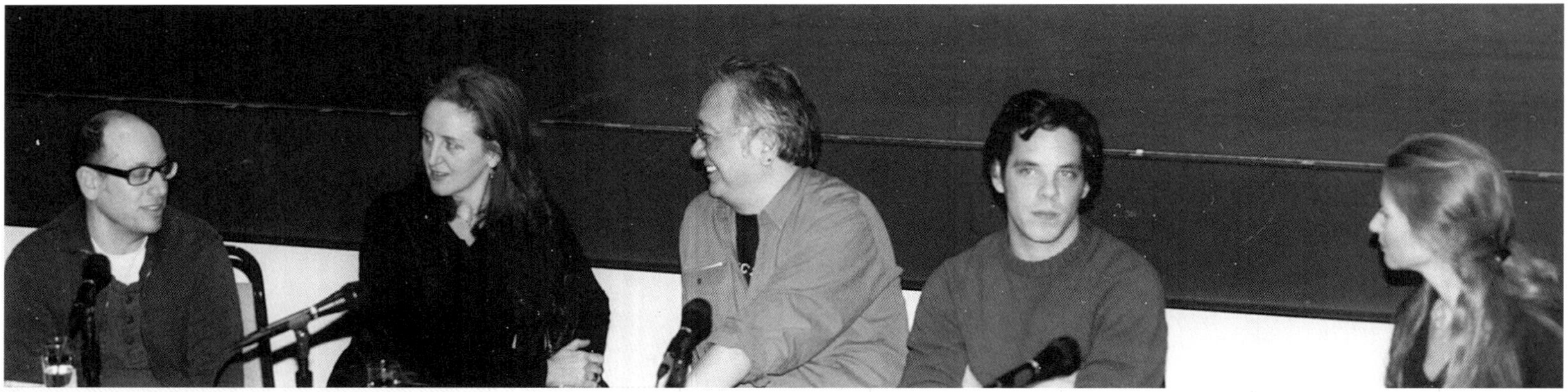

Left to right: David Brody, Lisa Stefanelli, John Yau, Christopher Francione, and Jennifer Riley.

On January 17, 2002, The Anderson Gallery of Virginia Commonwealth University's School of the Arts hosted a panel discussion as a prelude to the exhibition Young + Brash + Abstract. The panel was held at the Grace Street Theater and was attended by an audience in excess of two hundred students and faculty. John Yau was moderator, and four artists represented in the exhibition comprised the panel.

The following transcript is a record of their conversation.

John Yau: I just want to say a little about putting the show together. I don't think any curator is objective. We are all completely subjective, so I should sort of implicate myself in terms of what my subjectivity is.

I arrived in New York in 1974. I left Boston, Massachusetts, because I saw a Jules Olitski show at the Museum of Fine Arts in Boston and realized that that was as good as it was going to get in Boston. So I moved to New York. I'm a poet, and I also decided as a poet that I didn't want to work in a university teaching in an English department, which would limit my options as a poet. When I arrived in New York, I sold hotdogs at the South Street Seaport and looked at painting all the time, and kept a notebook. At a certain point in the mid '70s, I said to John Ashbery that I wished he would help me learn how to write art criticism, and he said "No, I'm not going to teach it to you. Why don't you just send an article to *Art in America*." So, in 1978, after a number of incidents, I ended up starting to write for *Art in America*. So I started writing about art at a time when abstraction was considered dead and painting was considered dead in many ways. And I guess, as a contrary person, if you decided to be a poet in America there's already something contrary about you, since as a poet, you can't make a living from your poetry; therefore, by American standards, you're a complete and utter failure. The notion of being contrary, I thought, would be useful in looking at art. And by that I meant that the more people who said painting was dead, the more I decided that they might be wrong. The more they said that abstraction had hit the end of the line, the more I realized that they were ignoring the actual situation.

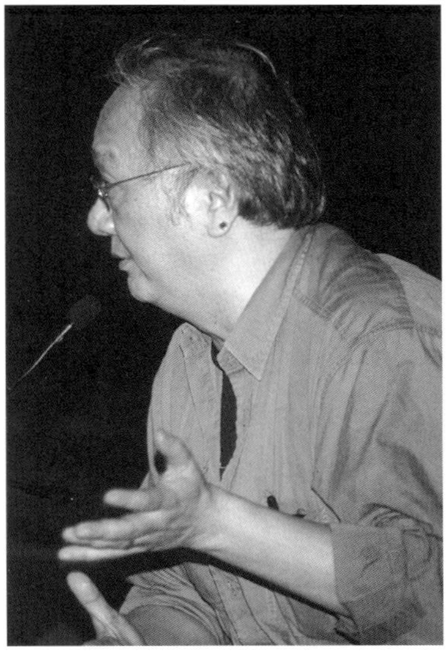

I've written about lots of different kinds of art. I think that there's a lot of received opinion in this country or in the world that you kind of accept. You know, "Andy Warhol's the greatest American artist," blah blah blah blah, and you kind of accept that without wondering what that means. Or the artist that sells the most work is the most successful person, or the most successful artist is the one who sells the most, which by that standard means that Sylvester Stallone is probably one of the greatest actors that the world has ever known. [*laughter*]

So I think there's a certain kind of value system that you have to kind of arrive at, that you know, you have to kind of...—Frank O'Hara, when he was asked his aesthetic, said, "If a man is chasing you down the street with a knife, you don't turn around and say 'Give it up: I'm a track star from Mineola Prep.' You kind of have to 'go on your nerve alone,' and I thought that that was really the aesthetic that I would stick by, whatever that means." Which sort of means that when you go to a party with a bunch of art critics, they go, "*You* wrote about *who?*" Things like that.

But anyway, when Ted Potter, director of Anderson Gallery, asked me to put this show together, I put it together going to galleries, remembering shows that I had been to, thinking about artists whose work I knew from different periods, and I didn't have a theory about abstraction or painting. And it was funny, I thought, "Oh, this show won't hold together at all because what I am thinking about won't be evident."

So here comes the subjectivity: on the way in from the airport, Ted says, "All the artists in the show are really control freaks, and they're really fussy."

And I was like, "Uh...."

"And they're all obsessed with surface, and they all draw, or have line in their work."

So my subjectivity was out in the open. For if Pollock was expansive and somehow history was deemed to have arrived at an end because, as Allen Kaprow said, "How do you go beyond Pollock?" In a way, these artists found the way to do it after the minimalist generation. They didn't empty it out: they found a way to put something back into the painting, or back into the field. And they did it in different ways, and I think I am of that period. I mean, I was born in 1950, so that I'm interested in what happens, say, from 1975, when I'm 25, on up to now. The other thing I would say about all the artists in the show is that they have a particular set of passions that don't compromise themselves with the culture's assumptions of what we're supposed to be passionate about. And in that sense, I think each of these artists go on their nerve alone, so I thought that's something you should kind of think about, that there's no one thing any one of you should like or work from or be influenced by. I mean, anyone can say, "Oh, well, I can write like John Cage," but it was John Cage who did it first. And I don't think it's that these people did it first, but that these individuals have the passion to be unabashed or unapologetic. I've always loved the fact that artists are unapologetic. That makes me secretly think that they're really poets, but that they just don't want to admit it.

So, I'll ask them a few questions that were handed to me, to just kind of get this started.

I know that two of them live in New York...one of them lives in Brooklyn, and we now consider that part of New York. When I first arrived in New York, I remember an artist saying, "Living in Brooklyn is like living in Ohio." Now it's like, living in Brooklyn is the only place to live. "Who wants to live in Manhattan?" is what one of the artists recently said to me. One lives sort of part-time in New York, and the other person is moving to New York after he goes to Japan. So I just wanted to ask them if they wanted to talk about why they moved to New York. Is it important? What did they think about it? Because it is a sort of lovely but impossible city. They're all nodding: lovely but impossible.

Lisa Stefanelli: I wouldn't call it lovely.

John Yau: Ok, just impossible. All right, you're all masochists. You all live in New York, and you have to hang this laundry out to dry.

Lisa Stefanelli: No, it's terrible. A lot of it is really, really terrible, and the only reason I'm there is because of my work. Period.

John Yau: Ok.

Lisa Stefanelli: I lived in Holland for a few years, and I was painting there, and it was so easy to be a painter in Amsterdam, because everyone was like, "Oh, you're a painter! Let me ask you about what you do!" For some reason, it was just a little too easy, and there wasn't enough adversity. And I think you need some challenge to be a good artist.

John Yau: What about the rest of you?

David Brody: First of all, I grew up in Brooklyn—

John Yau: But you must have left it...

David Brody: I was away for quite a while, but let me just tell you a story that might top the Ohio story. My mom recently told me that she gave birth to me in Manhattan Hospital so that it wouldn't say Brooklyn on my birth certificate. [*scattered laughter*] But, in fact, Brooklyn is home, but not where I currently live. After traveling around in Boston and California and other places, it wasn't until I literally set foot in Brooklyn that I realized there were actually other artists out there making paintings, and that I could talk to them about [paintings]. And that's pretty much it. That's why I'm there: because of the people.

And there's also a sense, in New York, since it's such a gritty.... it's a place that it doesn't matter if you make a mess, and there's a sense of independence that you can just go out and do what you want. I really get the sense, when I see people coming from Europe, and I just see their sense of "Wow! You can just grab some stuff off the street and bang it together and make a mess!" They don't have that kind of cultural freedom where they come from. And I think that's true about the suburbs. But also, one of the great things about New York is that there are people coming from all over, and they're the people that want to be there. So, of the artists that I know in New York, there's a very small minority that are actually from there.

John Yau: Right.

Jennifer Riley: I don't know if it's particular to New York, that kind of grittiness or what-not, because I spent a lot of time in Boston, and in a particularly gritty part of Boston, the South End, that's been undergoing a lot of reconstruction and a lot of new construction.

You know, the difference is, in Boston, there's a handful of people that you could really talk to about painting and about art on the level that you want to or need to. And in New York, it's multiplied. There's a dimensionality that doesn't exist pretty much anywhere else, and also New York's like the best place to see art. I mean, not that there isn't good art everywhere else, but the quantity and the quality, and the fact that it's completely always changing. It's very stimulating. I'm the one that's there part-time. "Part-time" because I have a life in Boston, and I've started a life in New York, and I still have a very deep attachment to a very large studio in Boston that hasn't yet been replaced. But if you want to keep learning and expanding and growing as a visual artist or as a non-visual artist, I think it's very important to be around a community that understands what language you're speaking, and that might even speak a different language that's inspiring and gets you out there.

Christopher Francione: I have to agree with you that it's mostly the community aspect of New York that sets it apart from other cities. I was in Chicago for a few years before I moved back east, and to me, the attitude of—as Jennifer said—you might find a handful of people that you might have something in common with or a dialogue, but in New York there's twenty fold of that. And the exposure to what we consider the art world is pretty direct when you're in New York. I go there pretty much every other weekend because I'm lucky enough to have friends who will put up with me although my studio is in Philadelphia. In some ways I'm lucky, because I don't live with the daily, kind of grind of New York, but to go there every other weekend is to stay in that community, and to see the current art scene as it unfolds, rather than catch it through a magazine. And I think that's important, to keep yourself moving as an artist.

John Yau: So, in a way, you're all really saying there's a painting culture in New York. I mean, I agree with [that], but it's also culture that's multiple or many-layered with many cultures within that culture.

Lisa Stefanelli: And it's so available. It's there, if you want it.

John Yau: Ok, I think we've answered all the questions I need to ask you. You're all so smart and articulate, eloquent. So, I thought I'd turn the questions over to the audience, and then I will field those questions and pass the little beach ball onto you.

Audience Member 1: When you were talking, all four of you talked about strategy, and game-playing in your own work, in some aspect. How much of the work comes from the idea that you're establishing your own set games, and how much of it would come from the idea that you're intermingling the games from art that you've seen and the daily culture that you're inside of and witnessing?

John Yau: The question is: What's the relationship between the game-playing that you initiate, and how much of it is derived from external sources? But it seems that I'm answering for all four, and they'll probably beat me up at dinner. That always happens to the curator. It's a little secret. The artists always get him into the closet and beat the crap out of him. Go ahead, Lisa.

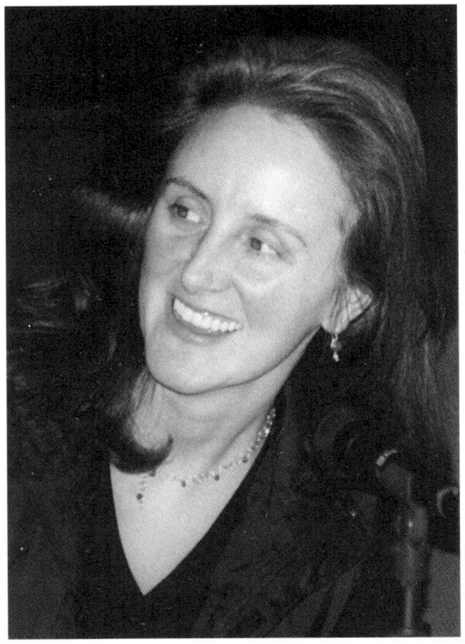

Lisa Stefanelli

Lisa Stefanelli: That question goes back to why we're in New York, pretty directly, actually. And it's a really good question, because sometimes I think that myself, and I wonder about living and working in a different community and how it would affect my work, and I know my work would be so much different if I wasn't constantly surrounded by a group of very intelligent and talented and active people.

So, I think that answers your question, right? It has a pretty big effect. Because human beings are social characters, social animals. We're classy mammals: that's all we are. And I don't think you can't not be affected by the community you live in.

> **John Yau:** Can I interject something? Don't you think the challenge in New York is almost more like on a daily basis, or a weekly, or a monthly than —

Lisa Stefanelli: What do you mean, like survival?

> **John Yau:** No, no. The challenge of like... you said it was an interesting community, but the challenge is literally going out and seeing a show, you know, one week and going "Oh".... That it seems constant and in a kind of interesting, inspiring, scary way, that that's what's real about New York.

Lisa Stefanelli: Well, maybe that's why I tend to hibernate sometimes, because it just gets too confusing.

> **John Yau:** Right.

David Brody: That's a paradox. I think if you're probably in a grad school program at a place like this, you're much more confronted with the self-consciousness of the games you are or are not playing. When you're in a place like New York, it's just so overwhelming, the culture of art out there, that it's a cliché of living in a metropolis. You actually have the freedom to be more of a loner and more on your own. Because you realize pretty quickly when you get there that you're not going to be an overnight art star, anyway. You don't have any crits coming up. No one, basically, gives a shit what you do, except a few of your friends, so you end up just doing it for yourself and a few of your friends. If something else happens out of that, that's great.

So, you know, I like being able to walk down the street and not have to interact with people, because I can act like I know where I'm going, and don't have to have conversation. That's the freedom you have in a larger city and not in a small town. That's comparable to being in a school as opposed to the art world, because you're on your own.

So, the kind of games that I play in my work are purely for my own amusement, and hopefully to produce something, to produce a problem that I can investigate. And the formal games that I'm playing are as old as everything, as old as civilization. Some of these guys are playing more directly with contemporary culture, and if you're looking at comic books, that's a different kind of a statement. I'm not sure what it means.

Christopher Francione: I think, with the question of whether or not you can isolate yourself from your surroundings or your peers and not appropriate from them, or lift from them, it's almost impossible. Sometimes I find myself overwhelmed by, or visually overwhelmed to the point where it's affecting my work. In that case, I tend to want to hibernate, and at other times, feel inspired where I need some kind of visual cattle prod. So, in respect to that, it's an interesting situation to not absorb so much, but yet to stay somewhat aware.

Grad school puts you in this tight scenario where you're in a critique, you're under the scrutiny of a magnifying glass to a degree. Once you leave the confines of that, you start to realize that what's important is that you're working for yourself, really, ultimately, and a small group of people that you relate to. Your peers become your springboard for dialogue. Much more so, for me, than I ever thought they would be.

Jennifer Riley: I'm thinking about that question a little bit differently—about how when you're saying how to play the game—and I was thinking about it in terms of how you structure your own work, and what kinds of problems you set up for yourself. From my point of view, I've looked at a lot of work, as much art history as I can ever look at, and also as much contemporary work as I can, and somewhere the work falls in between there.

You know, your own work comes out of a knowledge of what's happening and what has happened, and then if it's meaningful and it's really striking a chord with you, then it will come out. And I know that sounds a little esoteric, but I think it's really true, because things that glom onto you are the things that you're gravitating towards. And so the influence that you get sometimes from that kind of jolt when you see a show, and you just want to run home and borrow and try it out for a month or two, or a year or two, or whatever. That mindset or way of working may stick with you, or maybe it won't stick to you. I don't think there's any real way of deciding when and how long. You know.

Lisa Stefanelli: I want to ask the man who asked that question: why do you ask? Because I have to say, I didn't go to grad school. It took me five or six years to get over art school. [*laughs*] And I purposely didn't go to graduate school because I thought there would be too much fresh sort of direct criticisms and critiques. And in my mind, that would get way too much in the way. That's why the community I'm in right now is so great as opposed to an art school, because for me you can sort of bow out and not listen.

Jennifer Riley: Well, you only have to meet criticism halfway.

Lisa Stefanelli: Yes, but in art school, it's really imposed. More so, don't you think? Because you're paying attention and they care. Don't you think?

John Yau: I teach in the MFA program at Bard, and different writers, young writers, whatever, come there, and one student said something to Ann Lauterbach, what are you trying to teach us? And she said, "I'm not sure what I'm trying to teach you, but I'm trying to show you that you can build a community." And I thought that was actually a great answer. That you kind of go there, and maybe you meet some people, but that you leave that place, and you build a community out of your own generation. And I thought that's the best thing about grad school. But grad school can be New York City where you meet somebody next door, or down the block, or in a gallery, and that you build a sort of community of friends, and that the art world is built out of all of those communities, all of those communities sort of acknowledging that they're part of a larger community.

Audience Member 2: I guess this sort of got to be a New York love-fest.

John Yau: Well, that's because we don't live in Richmond.

Audience Member 2: I'm wondering if you ever thought about the fact that New York has such a provenance and there's such a critical dialogue that, in fact, it validates itself, so you really don't look outside. You don't see another point of view or another way of making art. I go to New York and see a lot of shows, and I'm always surprised at how many bad shows I see. And I go to other places, and I'm surprised at all the wonderful things I see.

John Yau: Well, I want to defend New York now. [*scattered laughter*] I think it's great that there are so many bad shows in New York. [*laughter*]

Because after all, Philip Guston, quoting a certain artist when the Soviets formed an artist's league, said: "You've given us everything. You've given us supplies. You've given us money. But you haven't given us the right to be bad." And I think, in a way, what I really love about New York is that there's lots of bad shows. But that's also true of any other city you go to—you say you're surprised by what's wonderful—is that what you're saying, that there's something wonderful in that city, but you're not acknowledging that there's lots of bad shows there. Because I was in Chicago, maybe four months ago, and I went to about twenty-five galleries, and I can't say that all twenty-five shows were wonderful. I would by lying. So....

Audience Member 2: Well, let me say that I think that the bad shows I saw, maybe I was one of the few people who thought they were bad.

John Yau: In New York? [*incredulously*] Come on, everybody who goes to New York... you just go to the right place, and you'll hear people grumbling about every show. There's probably two people that I really like, who are probably sitting somewhere saying, "I didn't think that Giacometti show was that good."

Come *on*. You're just carrying a kind of attitude here, if you ask me. [*scattered laughter*] I feel inclined to defend them.

Christopher Francione: As a person who doesn't necessarily live in New York, I think I can answer that in a certain way, because what would make me jump on Amtrak and pay that amount of money to go every other weekend? And maybe the amount and the frequency of artists and art shows, to a degree, makes it—not any more quality—but quantity to the point that, if you know where to go, you have the opportunity to see things that you wouldn't [see] in a smaller town. I lived in Chicago, and I saw lots of shows. But, you know, I can go to Chelsea and see 200 shows. There's a difference there that out of that many shows going on at once, I'm bound to find something I can bring away. So in that respect, not that I want to give New York gratitude unless it's due, but as a young artist, that's the place you keep your fire lit.

> **Audience Member 2**: You're not concerned that there's a certain kind of aesthetic that develops, a kind of Main Street New York aesthetic?

Christopher Francione: I don't know if there is one. If there is, I'm not aware of it. There's a diversity still there, to me. I don't find a certain style or a certain push towards one thing or another that doesn't exist in other cities as well.

David Brody: It's a marketplace. There's an understandable fallacy, if you're not in the middle of it, to think there's some kind of conspiracy located there that's directing what is considered to be modern art or contemporary art. If you're there, you'll realize that, as John was saying, the guy who's on the cover of *Artforum* this month is going to be hated by just as many artists in New York as loved. Because it's such an intense marketplace, it's a marketplace in terms of what gets sold and what gets bought. It's a marketplace in terms of ideas.

It's a marketplace in terms of trends. Everything is up against everything else. And if you went there with an anti-what-you-think-is-contemporary-art-attitude, you would have your place to say that. You would have to make your stand. Just like everybody else. And you might get a lot of recognition for that. But you're not going to get the recognition unless you go there and do it. You know, it's hard to do it unless you're there. That's what we're talking about: being there. That's the place to make your statement, and to see what people think.

Jennifer Riley: Yeah, that's a little different…I got into a discussion with some painters in Boston wanting to show only Boston people in a particular gallery, and they had this very "New York is the evil empire" kind of thing, and "everything is leaning towards New York, and we should show Boston because there's a lot of good stuff here."

Incidentally, for every one-eyed girl there's a one-eyed boy. So you can find what you want in New York, and you can find what you need here in Richmond, and you can find what you need in Boston, or what you like. And then there's what you don't like—not talking specifically to you, but in general—you might learn more from what you don't like than what you do like. But I was thinking about a symphony as a kind of art form that I don't think is site-specific. I don't think that a symphony is built for Manhattan or Chicago or London. That it transcends the geographical. And I think that good art can be found anywhere and transcends the geographical. The collection of what is available in New York is vital and stimulating.

Audience Member 3: I have a question. Why are you calling their work abstract when everybody's work that I saw... like Christopher directly lifted from comic-book imagery, the other two were talking about literary figures and narrative work, and David was the only one who actually talked about paint, and then his work makes reference with the landscape, so....

John Yau: So why am I calling the show "abstract"?

Audience Member 3: Yes.

John Yau: Well, I am questioning the word and making you think about that. You know, there's the notion that abstraction had to be pure abstraction in the '60s, but I don't think there's anything pure in the world. So the notion of abstract, I think, is probably in my mind a kind of hybrid. If you look at the work of someone like David Reed, you could say that they're pictures of paint strokes, his paintings, and in that sense they're not abstract, because it's a picture of something, at the same time that it is something. And I think that because I've had many conversations with David Reed and a number of other artists—Bill Jensen or Pat Steir—I realize they are altering the art world's definition of "abstract." I've learned more talking to artists certainly than from other critics.

In a way, I think the word "abstract" gets misunderstood. I think it's probably, at this point, a kind of hybrid possibility. It's not pure, and the space it defines is not representational.

So that's what I think, but you're certainly allowed to disagree with me. I'm sure you could publish something on it, and get it printed somewhere, and that would be great, because that leads to the dialogue of what's possible. "John Yau didn't know what he was talking about when he titled the show abstract for the following reason...." I mean, I'm being straightforward, because I think culture comes out of the dialogue, right, so my proposition to you is questionable, and you have a reason for it, and you could probably argue it out. The thing is, how does culture allow that to happen? Maybe it happens when you go to another studio with your friend and you go, "That guy didn't know what he was talking about for these reasons." But it gives you a kind of verbal permission and kind of clarity also about your own work. And that, I think, is what these people are talking about in terms of New York, just the conversation that arises out of looking at lots of work, and the conversations they have with other people, sort of sorting through and working those thoughts, enables them the possibility of a certain clarity. And I think that's useful.

Audience Member 4: Have the artists on the panel discussed why it's exciting for them to be painting, like today, in this period of time? Like, what they find exciting about what they do now?

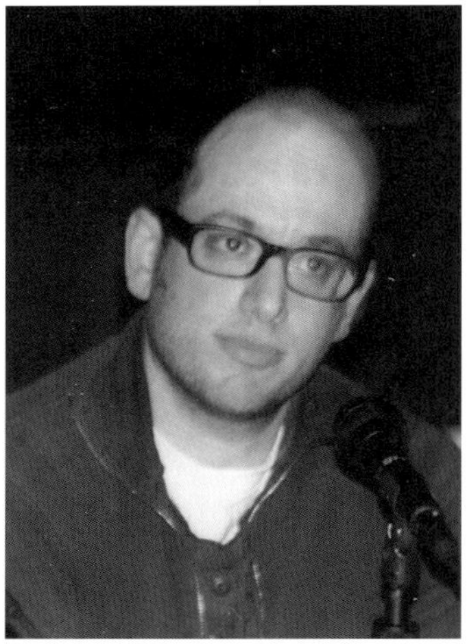

David Brody

David Brody: You mean when painting is dead?

Audience Member 4: Yes.

Lisa Stefanelli: I can say real quickly, that it's the thrill of the mystery of this very basic medium stretched, dragged, pushed, pulled across canvas. For me, I just never know what's going to happen next. Even though it might appear that.... because I work with interval and measurement and two or three different kinds of representation of abstracted space. Now, you'll have to figure out what I mean by that by going to the show. But it's just that: it's just the thrill and the mystery.

David Brody: To me, it's just the most advanced technology available. It's virtual reality. You can spend a lot of money on a computer that can't layer information as deeply as two paint strokes next to each other.

Lisa Stefanelli: I'm an incurable romantic.

Christopher Francione: I'm not a diehard painter. For me, it's whatever means necessary, and what the work calls for. I think I'm amongst more hard-core painters here on the panel.

John Yau: Yeah, we'll beat you up later. [*scattered laughter*]

Christopher Francione: For me, the romanticism of it, and the hierarchy of artwork, painting seems to reside on top, as something that I can engage and take seriously in a more devoted way, because it has such a long history. [*to Lisa*] Does that make sense?

Lisa Stefanelli: Yes.

Christopher Francione: Because you're laughing at it.

Lisa Stefanelli: No! I'm laughing at David with the technology comment. No, but for me, there's nothing else. I can't imagine that anything else would confront everything that there is for a human being to take in, in their life and in their world, through their eyes, through their ears, through their brain, everything. To me, painting is everything.

It's everywhere. It's under the glass. It's at night when I go to sleep. I don't know. It answers everything for me. Do I sound like I'm going to start a cult? [*laughter*] No, it's everything.

John Yau: That makes sense.

Audience Member 6: Everyone seems to mention this dialogue that takes place from the folks on the street and this kind of density. And I found it kind of interesting that here you are, a poet, and you're looking at visual arts now, and from the perspective of a writer, and it seems that as you're talking about painting, I'm curious about this dialogue that takes place. So I'm wondering if you're all involved in other things, whether it's literature or psychology or physiology, and having a dialogue with folks on the street having to do with issues in addition to making marks on bits of canvas.

John Yau: You mean, who else do I hang out with?

Lisa Stefanelli: Well, there's no reason to be interested in anything else if you're an artist. [*laughs*] No, I mean, for *me*, everything's about painting. I mean, *everything*. You know, of course, I love to write, and I love to do everything, but it all comes together through paint.

John Yau: I don't think that's what he meant. I think what he meant is that you paint, but there are other kinds of things that you're talking with. You know, literature, poets, whatever. One of the things, at least in my experience with New York... you know, a certain book, like everybody will read it and then start talking about it. And there are phases. Like, there's the book about the right brain and the left brain, and you couldn't go to a party without someone talking about that book. And then James Gleick writes about chaos, and you couldn't go to a party.... And I think that's part of the dialogue, because all of those things have to do with perception, right? I mean, in a way, all of those books were talking about how the mind works and perception. And so, in a way, those books become the sort of groundwork for other possible conversations or investigations. I think that's one thing that happens. Probably in every community.

Arthur Danto said that painters have better parties than poets. [*laughter*] But I go to both. I actually like to have parties where I mix it up, and I throw the poets in with the painters, the painters in with the poets. I arrived in New York with the image of Frank O'Hara hanging out at the Cedar Bar, disillusioned to discover that the Cedar Bar wasn't really the Cedar Bar anymore, [that] poets and artists didn't really hang out as much as they used to. But I still hang out with a lot of artists and writers.

David Brody: It's a little unfair, because one of the roots of a dialogue between poets and writers and artists is the traditional one in which poets write art reviews. There's no equivalent way for painters to comment on poetry, and most painters don't really know what's going on in contemporary poetry except [by] a little bit of osmosis. I lived for many years with a poet, and we didn't talk much about poetry. I got to go to a few poetry readings that I wouldn't have gone to otherwise and heard some stuff that I wouldn't have been exposed to. My impression is that, since your generation perhaps, there's been an academicizing of—whatever that word is—of poetry just as there is of art, because it's taught in schools now. The people that were hanging out in the Cedar Bar now go to grad school.

John Yau: Right.

David Brody: So, there's a bit of a gulf there. But just by association, there's stuff that happens, and I think there's been a bit of a shift. I see more artists writing in literary journals, and more poets writing about art and actually doing art, looking at art. I think that's a good thing.

Lisa Stefanelli: I think the place to talk to other artists or find other artists, first of all, is at openings, and then you see, you find the artist whose work you like, and then you go up and you say, “Hey, I like your work. We should talk some time.” And then you find your micro-family within that other family. But then there are the incidents of life that put you in the orbit of somebody who happens to become a friend, who’s like a biologist or physicist or something like that, and then you meet their best friend, who’s a political scientist who writes about Israel, Pakistan, and all the Middle East issues.... You know, it just kind of goes on and on. I wanted to answer your question about what other things I like. I like art! I like sculpture. I like music. I like science. I like string theory. I mean, if I find somebody that wants to talk about that, that’s great!

Audience Member 5: Actually, what I was asking was, are there issues in these pictures that are influenced by things other than painting?

Lisa Stefanelli: All of the above.

John Yau: I mean, I think all of them confessed to a certain autobiography: being a figure skater, loving literature, being an incurable romantic. One isn’t necessarily born an incurable romantic. One elects to become an incurable romantic and pay the price for it, right? So, I think in a way they all were influenced by something other than art. Art is the place where all those other possibilities get alchemically transformed, and it’s the way they get to reflect upon their experience without being, you know, transparently autobiographical and writing a memoir. Because maybe that’s not what they want to do. Somehow painting has this thing right about it.

I mean, how do you explain being a poet? You’re this guy who sits in a room and fiddles around with thirty-six words for three weeks and thinks it’s the greatest thing since the last time he fiddled around with that limited vocabulary. [*scattered laughter*] And your wife says, “Don’t you want to go out?” And you go, “No. I want to fiddle around with these thirty-six words that I’ve chosen to write a poem using only this vocabulary.”

I think it’s pleasure. That’s what Lisa and I talked about before the piano started. The real secret to painting that nobody wants to deal with is that there’s a certain kind of pleasure that one gets from it and that one gets doing it. Certainly for me as a poet, that pleasure is irreplaceable. I have other desires. I’m certainly not monkish about being a poet. This is a pleasure I don’t want to put aside only for other pleasures.... eating hotdogs.

Audience Member 7: I'm curious about the term "brash."

John Yau: Brash?

Audience Member 7: Brash, as the quality that these four, and all the other painters you've chosen have. For me, when I think about that quality, that there's a certain rejection or act of criticism in the larger academy, specifically in this case in painting.

And you've talked a lot about community tonight, and after seeing the work, I'm just curious...how, as the curator, if you could tell us a little bit about how these particular artists that you've selected are sort of actively engaging in a discourse in painting that would be brash in comparison to other painting that's being made today.

John Yau: I would say the first thing.... There are two answers to this question. One is that Ted called me up and asked me for a title, and I took the Allen Ginsberg "first thought, best thought," which I don't usually do. So I said, okay, I'll come up with a title, and as I was drinking my coffee, I said, "young, brash and abstract." I thought it had a nice ring to it. Doesn't sound like a law firm. [*laughter*] So, it had a ring to it; otherwise, you wouldn't have asked me the question. You'd just see the title, and you'd see through it, and then it would be meaningless. I like the idea of attaching brash to abstract, because people may not think of it as being brash, anymore. You know, it has a long history, this and that.

And the third thing I thought is that there's something brash about wanting to be a painter in the 21st century. And you might not think so, but if you've lived in New York, it's repeatedly said painting is dead. I don't know if you know the work of Hal Foster, art theorist. "Painting is bourgeois activity. How could you be a painter?" Of course, he's teaching at Princeton, probably being paid $100,000 a year, and driving around in a nice car. Hey, we won't question that. But the notion that painting is a bourgeois activity, which is something that was really said a lot in the '70s and the '80s when I first got to New York and when I first started writing, seemed really intriguing to me. Because if you think about it, it costs more to make a Jeff Koons or a Matthew Barney than it costs to make a painting.

So what's truly a bourgeois activity? A painting can be done on an old bed sheet, as Jasper Johns did his first flag painting on, using some wax and pigment and some newspaper. I don't think it really costs a lot of money. And I would also suggest to you that if you put the works of Jasper Johns, despite whatever their price is, up, and the works of Frank Stella up, as Frank Stella becomes more successful, his work costs more to make. So in a way, he's identified more with his audience: the wealthy collector. Whereas Johns, the work doesn't cost more to make, so if you're a young artist and you go into a museum or a gallery and you see his work, you may not become immediately alienated. Whereas if you go to see a Damien Hirst bronze statue that stands fifteen feet high, you might say, "Well, how the hell am I ever going to become an artist?" And as a poet who is stuck with the poverty of words, probably one of the reasons I like painting is that I feel like it's one of those activities where you accept the limitations, and you take on the burden of history, and you're not freaked out by it, and that there's something brash about that.

It's *less* brash, to me, to have enough money to make a twenty-foot-high bronze sculpture and to have a lot of assistants, than to go into your studio and make a painting. So that's why I called the show *Young + Brash + Abstract*. The word "young" I picked because I decided that anyone—I was born on June 5th, 1950—that anyone who was born on June 6th, 1950, or after, is young. And abstract, as I said earlier, is to evoke "what does that word mean now?" given its whole historical content and definition through time. It has to do with making a space with paint, a place where speculation can begin.

Audience Member 8: I had a question for the artists when they were talking... about play and strategy, it seems to me that you're verging on gimmicks and formulas: pour a bunch of latex paint and outline it, and do that ten times, and you have a show. Is it a case of...finding a formula and then reproducing it over and over again?

John Yau: The question is when does play become formulaic and when can it still be open-ended?

Lisa Stefanelli: I can answer that. As soon as you start getting money for your paintings. [*scattered laughter*]... I think that I've come to this really profound conclusion in the last two years, since I had my first sell-out show: it's so dangerous to start getting paid to make paintings. Incredibly dangerous. And you just have to be really careful about these things. If you're serious about being an artist, you're not going to get formulaic, well, in a formulaic way. You have to be really careful. But anyone who knows how to be an artist knows how to watch out for that sort of thing. Right?

John Yau: Yeah.

Jennifer Riley: I was thinking that it sounds like you're saying understanding a strategy is kind of a bad thing and that somehow figuring out a way to comment on—and I think that's kind of an important part of the educational process as an artist—is to understand the strategies before you, and either find a way to, a, comment on them, or b, incorporate them in a new way, in a way that only you can make them new and fresh and vital and honest.

David Brody: I think there's a spectrum, and on one end you have formula and on the other end you have chaos, and to make art you need both. You need something that has some kind of a focus, and if you don't have an understanding of formula, you don't have form. You need form to make art.

Audience Member 9: This has been touched on. I'm a painter. I've been painting for decades, and people have been saying that painting is dead and so forth. I'm wondering, for you four as artists, how connected do you feel to a tradition of painting, and how important is it for you as painters to be adding something to that tradition? Your talks were all sort of mercifully bereft of theory, and you only mentioned a couple of artists. More and more, I read art criticism about painters where they say, "These painters don't seem to care that painting is dead. They just like to paint." And they talk about it from there. And I'm wondering, because Mr. Yau mentioned that he liked unapologetic artists, I wonder if that's how you see yourself. Or if it's even something that enters your mind?

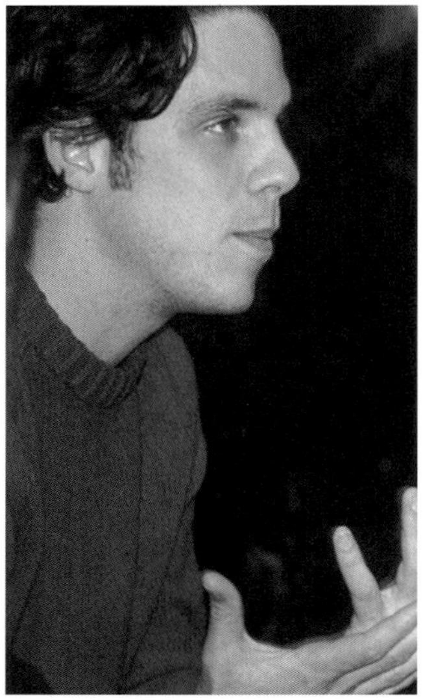

Christopher Francione: As far as the history of painting goes, I think it's important for painters to be aware of it. Whether or not they're adding to it, I think that's a goal when you make a painting...to do something kind of uncategorized in that history or in that canon, but for me.... I might be the wrong person to answer, because I don't like being called a painter. I don't engage in the dialogue of painting as much as maybe the people next to me do. I'm more interested in a more universality about making work. And that's for me. Most people will disagree with me when I take that kind of attitude, but as far as the dialogue of painting and criticism [is concerned], I mean we all went through the motions of having a dialogue about theory, but it's there, but it seems to not be pertinent for me in a conversation about my work. I think it can be applied by an outsider. I'm aware of certain critical theory, but I tend to stay away from thinking about it in the current time of working. It tends to be a crutch for me to consider it during the process. In retrospect, maybe, it's healthy to accept.

So to say that we don't or I don't care about that, I do care, but I'm just a little more aloof about it, to a degree. Maybe more so than others.

David Brody: I just look at painting. I love painting. I've looked at it for many, many years, since I was a kid. Last week, I was in Philadelphia, and I went to the Pennsylvania Academy and looked at the collection there, and frankly, the paintings I was interested in there were by fairly forgotten... like the Hudson River School of painters, that sort of thing. It's just fascinating to me, to look at paintings. I think it would be really stupid to strategize—at least for me, the way I work—to strategize about where I'm going to place myself in that history, because if you start thinking in that way, you're going to cut your own throat. You just can't do anything. So, when I'm working on my paintings, I'm just working on my paintings, and they have their own logic and their own path. But if you're a painter, you're looking at paintings all the time.

There is no history of painting: that's a complete fiction. There's just a lot of paintings out there that people have been making for a long time, and what looks like a monolithic march of progress, in fact, is a war that's just been going on as long as there've been people making paintings. So you can pick and choose from among that, jump through time, and you can hate Rembrandt, and you can love Sanford Gifford. It's up to you.

> **Jennifer Riley:** Like Lisa, I think I'm very romantic about my approach, but I also feel I have a molecular attachment to paint now that I've been working with it for so long. I might be becoming myopic or something, but I think everything is painting. Everything that isn't exactly built and constructed I see as painting....
>
> If painting is dead, how come everybody is putting paint on their sculpture?

Lisa Stefanelli: I'm an incurable romantic. I mean, I'm addicted to any kind of historical painting, but not even just like Rembrandt or going to Barcelona to see the paintings that Picasso made as a 12-year-old that just blow your mind, but also I would give anything to be able to walk onto a shipyard in the 1920s and check out the lead-base paints and see what it looked like when they first applied them. That stuff is really, really interesting to me. I don't know if this answers your question or not.

As far as art history goes—which I think is probably what you're more interested in knowing about—I think I'm more interested in the history of paint, and it just happens that there's this weird gene pool of people who work with it that are called painters, and historically, they're kind of interesting, because of that.

Audience Member 10: Do you guys like Thomas Kincaid?

John Yau: Who?

Audience Member 10: Thomas Kincaid.

John Yau: I've never heard of him.

Audience Member 10: You've never heard of him?

John Yau: No.

Audience Member 10: He's the painter of light.

John Yau: He's the painter of light? That's probably why I've never heard of him. I thought Monet was the painter of light.

Jennifer Riley: You hear him in the elevator as Musak.

David Brody: On some level, anything is interesting. One of my fantasies is to curate a show of the top ten best selling artists of the past year of original art, and obviously Thomas Kincaid would probably be number one, maybe Jasper Johns would be number two in terms of total sales. I don't know.

John Yau: LeRoy Neiman. Come *on*....be reasonable.

David Brody: I don't know. He seems to be slipping. It certainly would have been true ten years ago, but he might still be up there. It will be interesting to find out. You know, hack into the IRS and find out who really made the most money as an artist, and then you'd have a completely objective evaluation of what art is, because if I try to sit here and tell you why I think Thomas Kincaid is a terrible painter, I'd sound like an idiot. So the only thing to really do is to say, "Well, he's a great painter," blah blah blah. So, I think he's a great painter.

Jennifer Riley: Do you like him? [*addressed to audience member*]

Audience Member 10: Yeah.

Jennifer Riley: Why?

Audience Member 10: It's so nice that he's so unapologetic. [*laughter*] I just think it's interesting that he believes in it.

John Yau: I know, but I find it interesting that you say that he believes that, because this is a country of religious cults, and you could convince anybody to believe— You could get three people together and start a religion tomorrow, you know, in which you worship the hotdog roll. And somebody is going to say, "Well, I really like that guy because he believes in that, and that's interesting." Or you could say, "Well, okay." So I mean, I think... well, never mind. I won't go there. Ted asked me to be nice.

Audience Member 11: I'm just wondering, because everyone has been talking about playing games and stuff in your work, and this idea of trying to set up problems for yourself that you thought were interesting....

I'm just wondering, how do you gauge being too self-indulgent and keeping other people's interests peaked?

Lisa Stefanelli: Well, I'm absolutely interested in having people at least find something in my work.

Audience Member 11: Like, if you paint the color red.

Lisa Stefanelli: Well, you know, I listen to people when they talk about what they dig or don't dig, you know? I mean, it's not like it's going to make me completely change, but I think human beings just like to be social. I mean, somehow it makes sense to say that.

Audience Member 11: Well, I guess it's just that, with all the questions, and talking about all the pressures, it seemed like you were saying, "Oh, I can walk down the street, and I don't have to pay attention, and I don't have to talk to anybody," but then there's this whole idea of living in a community of your peers. So how do you gauge when you're too self-indulgent? So, how do you figure out when someone else is going to care?

John Yau: So, it's the relationship between the outside and the inside, right?

Audience Member 11: Yeah.

David Brody: The only way that anyone is going to care about what you do is if you are infinitely self-indulgent.

Lisa Stefanelli: Mm-hmm.

David Brody: Because, you know, you make something that you care about, and you want to make it the way you want to make it. That's the only way that you're ever going to make that communication. So, if you mean by self-indulgence just being lazy—that's how it's often used—

I'm not talking about that. I'm talking about the kind of self-indulgence where you wanna make what you wanna make, and you don't care what anybody else thinks. Then, when you've made that piece, you'll be surprised, because then people will care about it.

Jennifer Riley: But also, if people respond to your work, if you cast your work out there and people look at it, and they have an experience while looking at it, and they respond to it, in a positive or negative way—hopefully, for the most part, positive—and it strikes a chord with your intentions sometimes, sometimes not, you learn from their experience, which is totally out of your control. But a lot of times, you get their response to your work which is kind of what you're trying to do. You're in this because you're trying to communicate something on a very, very deep level, something that....

Well, I'm speaking for myself, [since] I don't consider my work [to be] particularly glib. When somebody has an experience with my work that they relate to me, that's the best reward. Then I know that, in David's terms, I'm being appropriately indulgent, because I'm not responding to somebody's positive criticism and making a body of work based on that. I'm making a body of work based on my response to their response to my response to my own work, and so on, and so on, and so on.

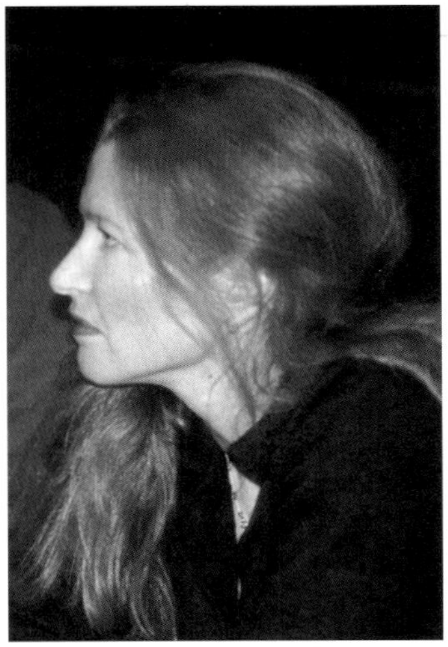

John Yau: I think self-indulgence is one of those words that people say to artists or writers. You know, you're just being self-indulgent. You're not doing anything to contribute to the community, because you actually get the pleasure of going to your room and being by yourself, and everybody distrusts the person that goes to his or her room and stays there for long hours. "What's that person cooking up in there?" And when you're a kid, it's great, because, oh, he or she's in their room and they're not making any noise. But then when you get a little older, like 25, and you're still in your room not making any noise, people think, "Oh, shit, what's going on in there?" So there's that part of being self-indulgent, and it's used in a sort of puritanical way, I think. It's a way to make yourself feel bad about being an artist. Like, oh, you want to be an artist; that's so self-indulgent.

You wanna be Tom Hanks. To me, that's pretty self-indulgent. The guy makes 18 million dollars. What does he do?

Audience Member 11: He's turning down roles. Since he's getting paid, there's a certain danger, when the money rolls in, of being self-indulgent.

John Yau: I don't think painting is that self-indulgent, because it seems to be that it's hard to be a painter. You know? I mean, just the practical...I mean, every painter I've ever met, whether they were successful or not, didn't say, "Ah, that was easy! I'll go in and do another one!" [*scattered laughter*]

You know? I mean, you don't want to bring in the word "suffering." I mean, come on: there's real people suffering, but it doesn't seem like it's that easy, either. They're struggling. They're struggling to do something that often eludes *me*. I mean, they wanna do *what?* I think that's interesting.

Christopher Francione: Well, I took your question to mean more about maybe complacency in the work, whereas you make a body of work where you stick to your guns about maybe a process. Are you saying where is that exhausted and where is it not? Is that what you're ...?

Audience Member 11: Well, I was just taking into account other questions that have been asked up to this point.

Christopher Francione: I think I have a paranoia about being complacent, and maybe that shows in some of my slides. I work on this kind of aspect coming from different angles, and that's maybe a shortcoming of mine, or maybe it's a difference that I might have amongst other people. I think people have different levels of what they can commit to, and how rigidly they're going to expose themselves in that medium or process. I think that people just have a different level about how committed they are to one thing. And some people's minds work differently, so that, really, the result is all over the place.

So, in respect to that, to complacency about work, I think some people have a shorter attention span than others about what they get involved with. And, to the criticism of some people, I think that people lock onto a process that seems to be working for them, and they exhaust it to the point where you wonder why they continue. That's a question I think everybody asks themselves, whether they're finished with that, but I guess that's really for the artist to decide, hopefully, whether they feel like they're kicking a dead horse. I don't know.

David Brody: You also have to cultivate people whose eye and mind you respect, so that if person X says, "Oh, that painting sucks. Why are you doing that?" I might completely disregard it, but if person Y said that, you know, I might think about it. Because, based on a track record, based on their work and my experiences with them, I'm going to listen to what they say. I might throw it out, and I might say, "Well, you just don't get it yet." I might take that back into the work. So, you have to be selective in terms of who you're listening to and you develop that with time.

[*audience member's question could not be discerned. John fields the question....*]
He's wondering if self-indulgence can limit an artist and in what ways.

Christopher Francione: Yes, I think we went down a path where we might have portrayed it as people who don't think of that, for some reason, but I think my surroundings and commentaries from my peers very much would drive me to make work, and I consider it on a daily basis. I'm not one who doesn't have to answer to anything. I have the academic training and a sort of confidence about it where I feel I need to answer to those things, not disregard them. I don't think anyone here disregards their surroundings, their peers, or any critical kind of aspect that they might be able to get about their work.

David Brody: Personally, I think...I mean, I know where that question's coming from, and I feel like, yeah, you're always faced with this question of are they just not getting it? Or do I need to be even more stubborn? Or am I just digging myself into a black hole? And you just have to answer that in the work all the time. The answer is in the work.

Jennifer Riley: I have one additional comment. If, on the particular occasion, this person is an absolute genius, nobody understands that person, maybe, and the other possible situation is that the person is actually in the wrong group. You know, say the person has grown, and they're in a different place, and the people who are giving that person criticism, maybe they haven't grown, or maybe it's just a different mind-set. One could be in the wrong place. One could be in the wrong school, for instance. I'm not saying anybody here is in the wrong place, but like I said earlier, you have to meet criticism halfway. You accept the mantle of being a student, which is to be open and receptive and throw it out if it doesn't work, and keep it if it does. You know, whatever you throw out, at least keep a photocopy of it so you can look at it later.

David Brody: I think what I was trying to remember is that the important thing is that you don't *withdraw* because you're getting criticism that you don't agree with. I mean, if you're doing something that's stubborn and everyone disagrees with it, it might be that you're onto something. And the important thing is to keep putting it out there and see if it stands up to the criticism. And I know this because I withdrew for a long time when I was painting, because no one was interested in looking at my paintings. And they probably were really bad, and that's just as well, because it took me a while to get to a place where I could throw stuff out there and say I don't care what you think. When I did that, I found that there are people that are going to be interested in the work, if it's got something.

So, be stubbon, if you need to be, but that doesn't [equal] withdrawal. Put it out there, and let's see what the criticism does to it.

John Yau: Ok, that's a nice place to end.

Artists' Statements +

Exhibition Reproductions

[Walter Biggs]

My work investigates the spiritual and alchemical associations of particular precious and non-precious materials, their appearance—real or artificial—and the use of reflection as a pictorial device.

The paintings I create offer the viewer a paradox: their presence suggests a type of order and complexity found only in nature. Conversely, their actual making denies that origin, creating an inexplicable balance between what is real and what is not.

Graphite, mica, pigment, sand, and oil are the makeup of my work. Through repetitive brushwork and the spontaneous mixture of materials directly on a support, I create a picture plane. Then, by scraping and coating, polishing and manually arranging my materials, I work the surface until all traces of touch are gone.

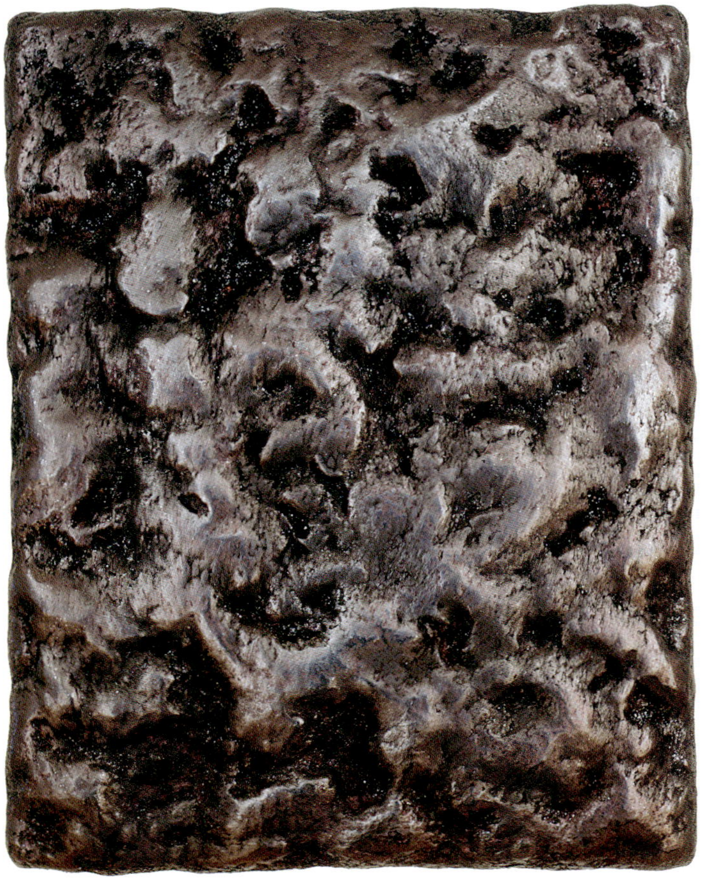

Lava
1992-93

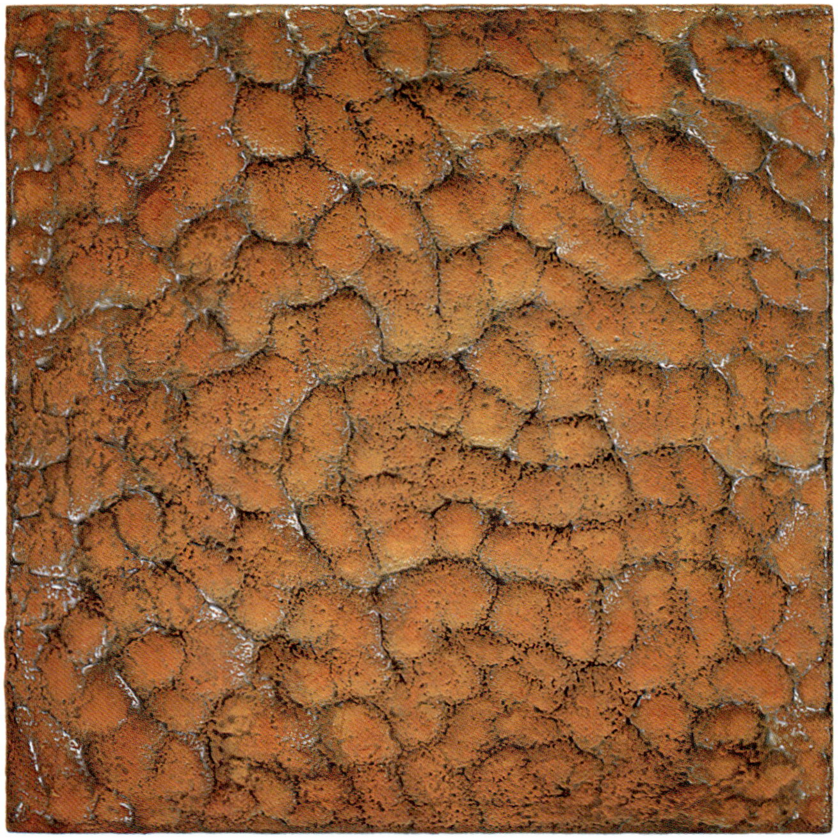

Red Devil
2001

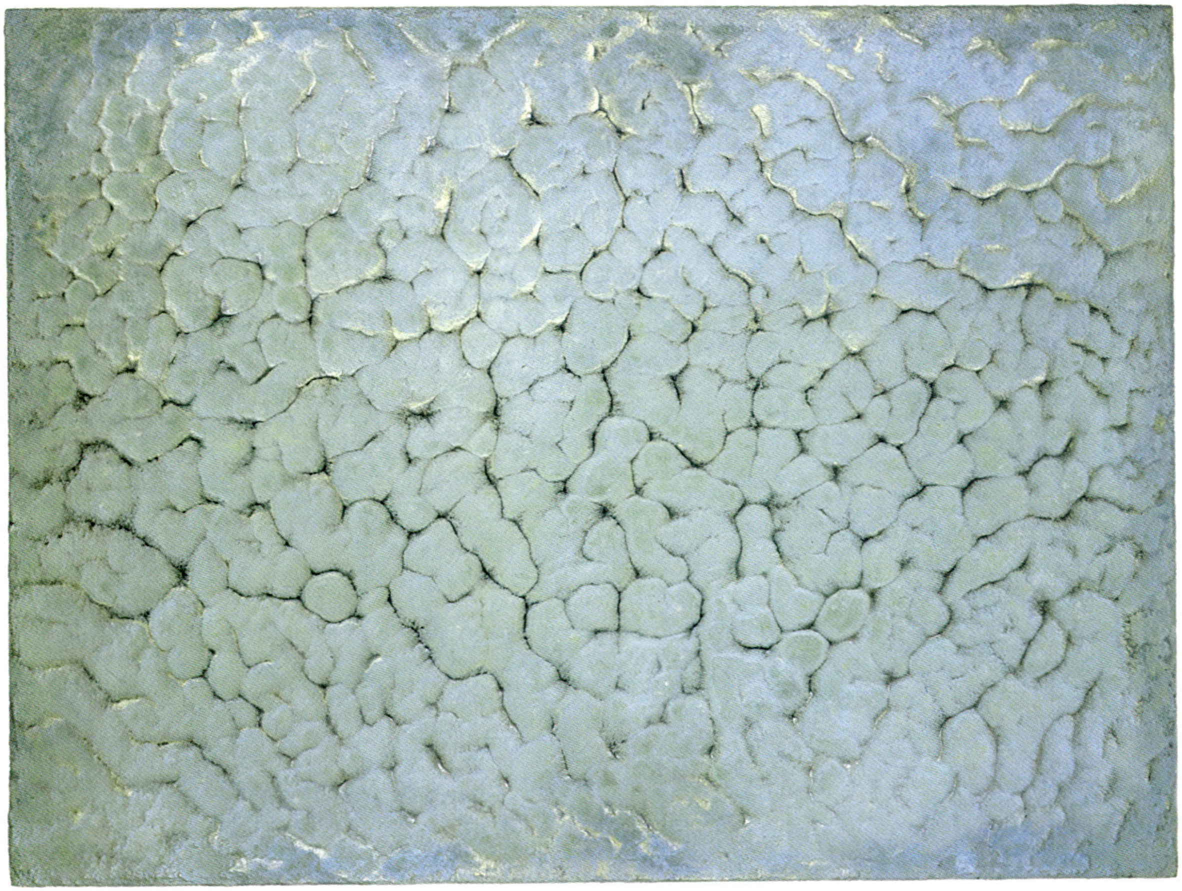

Water Painting
1998-99

David Brody

I make paintings and drawings. The paintings use chalk lines to establish a perspective space with vanishing points. The drawings use an isometric spatial grid, no vanishing points.

The two bodies of work talk to each other but can't touch. When I make paintings I don't begin with any images or drawings or ideas. I wouldn't know how. As marks accumulate, they define each other spatially—sort of. I suppose this openness is one of the things that is meant by abstract painting.

As carefully as possible, I get rid of things that don't matter or don't work; anomalies, accidents, and contradictions are what the painting grows out of. But I do get rid of things. Color, irrational and improvised like everything else, sneaks up and becomes the most telling problem. If the painting works as a painting in the end—color, space, light—it hints at pattern and order. If it works, it suggests all sorts of ideas and pictures.

The drawings are the exact opposite of the paintings. Beginning with the isometric grid, the same everywhere, they take pattern and order as a given and suggest complications. The drawings argue that the world is made *this* way.

Sometimes I work with the mathematical idea of recursion, like a homemade fractal, but in fact it's not so mathematical. As the drawing grows out of its own procedure, new decisions have to be made that were never thought of at smaller scales. Aesthetic decisions. A procedure is never finished defining itself. A drawing is not a machine.

Most of the drawings, though, are not recursive. They do contain levels of symmetry—as many levels as possible—but they are not mathematically grown. Symmetry, by the way, is a fluid concept. Think of a person losing a leg, then joining up with someone who's lost the other leg: symmetry within asymmetry within symmetry. This is how music works. I call my drawings *Fragment of a Much Larger Thing* because I want to suggest how the whole world can be made by this kind of thinking—that it's just a matter of scale.

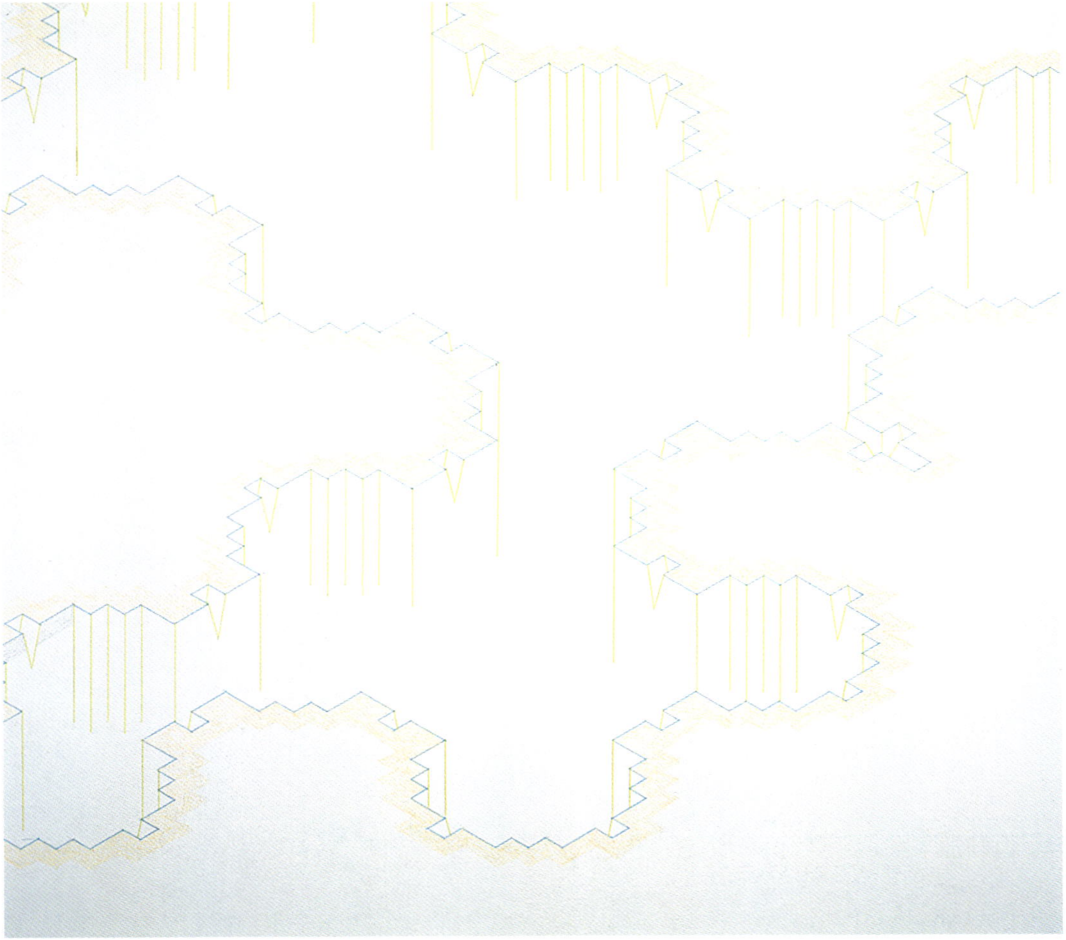

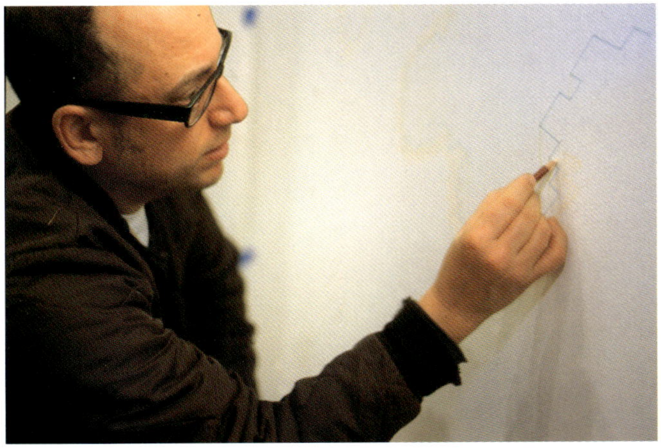

Fragment of Much Larger Thing: Reticulum
2002

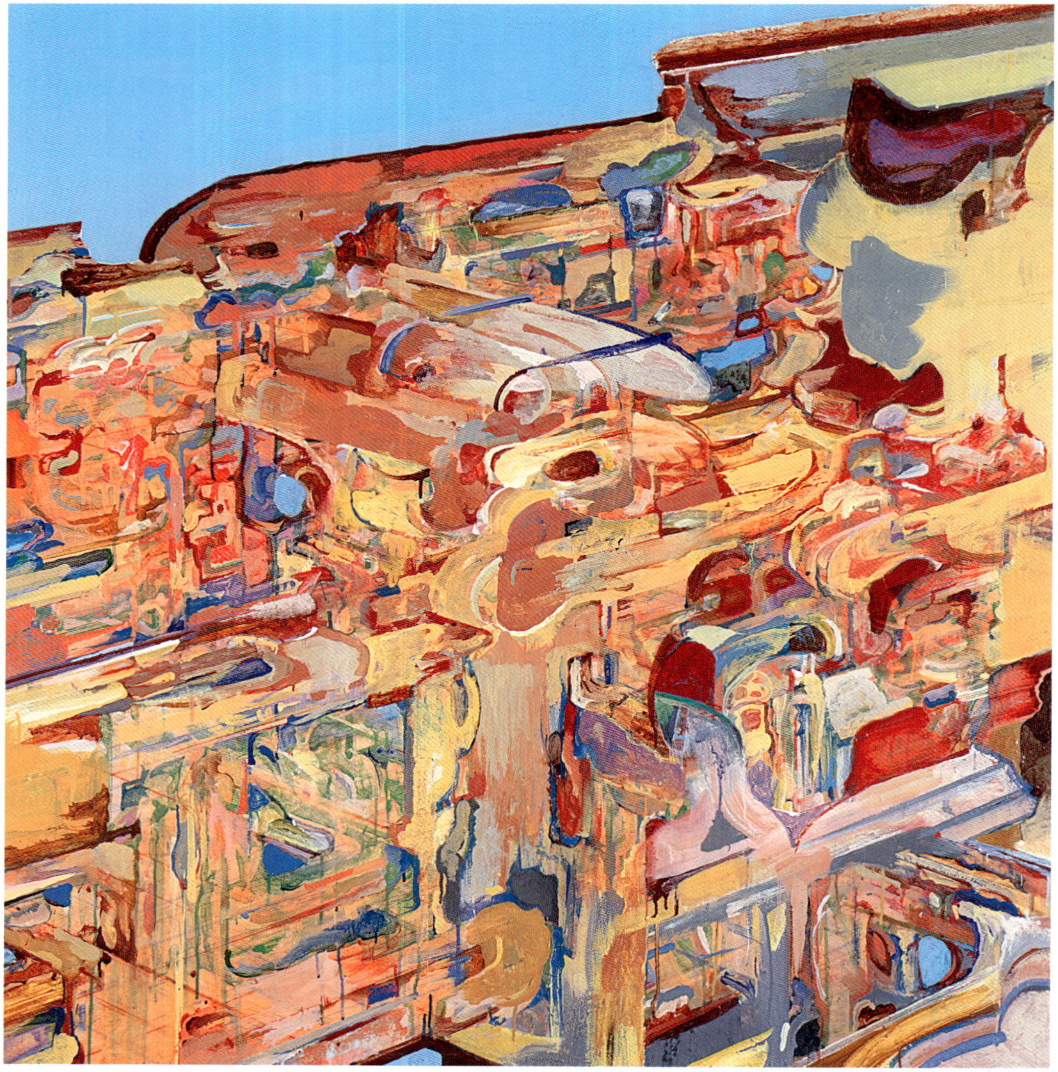

Region 36
2000

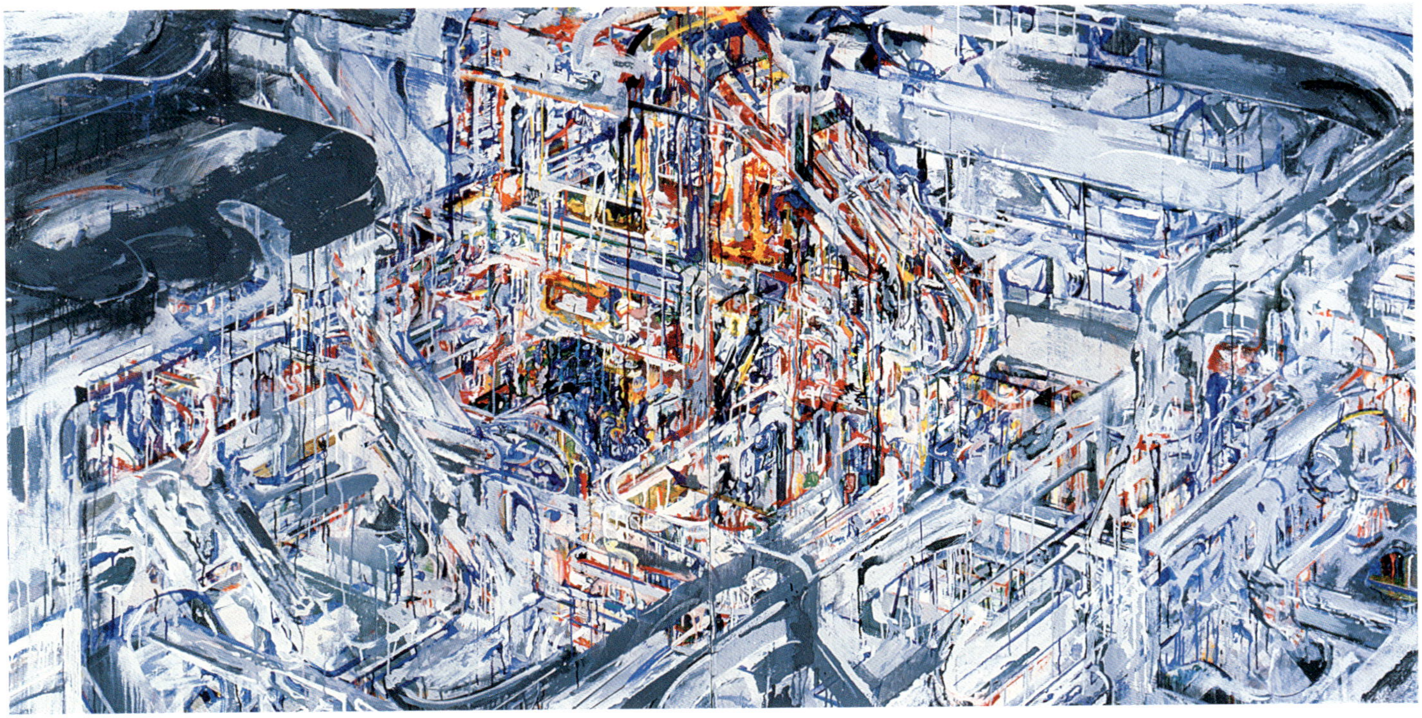

Region 32
1998

[Henry Brown]

I describe my work as mechanically drawn geometric abstractions. Taking a scientific and investigative approach, I use a visual language of geometry and mathematical principles to construct painted images.

On the surface of each painting I draw a schematic and use it to form the contours of the geometric image. I paint in the image, leaving the schematic exposed to function as a pictorial element in the finished work. The image appears to be static or in stasis, but a sensation of movement and animation carries the viewer's eyes across the painting's surface.

Variations in line quality, eccentricities in the painted edge, and graduations in the knifed finish of the gessoed layer show evidence of the hand in the application of materials and mechanical processes. Lines and marks inscribed on each painting's surface document the thought process and methodology of the accompanying geometry, and supplement the colored image to form a comprehensive unit of meaning.

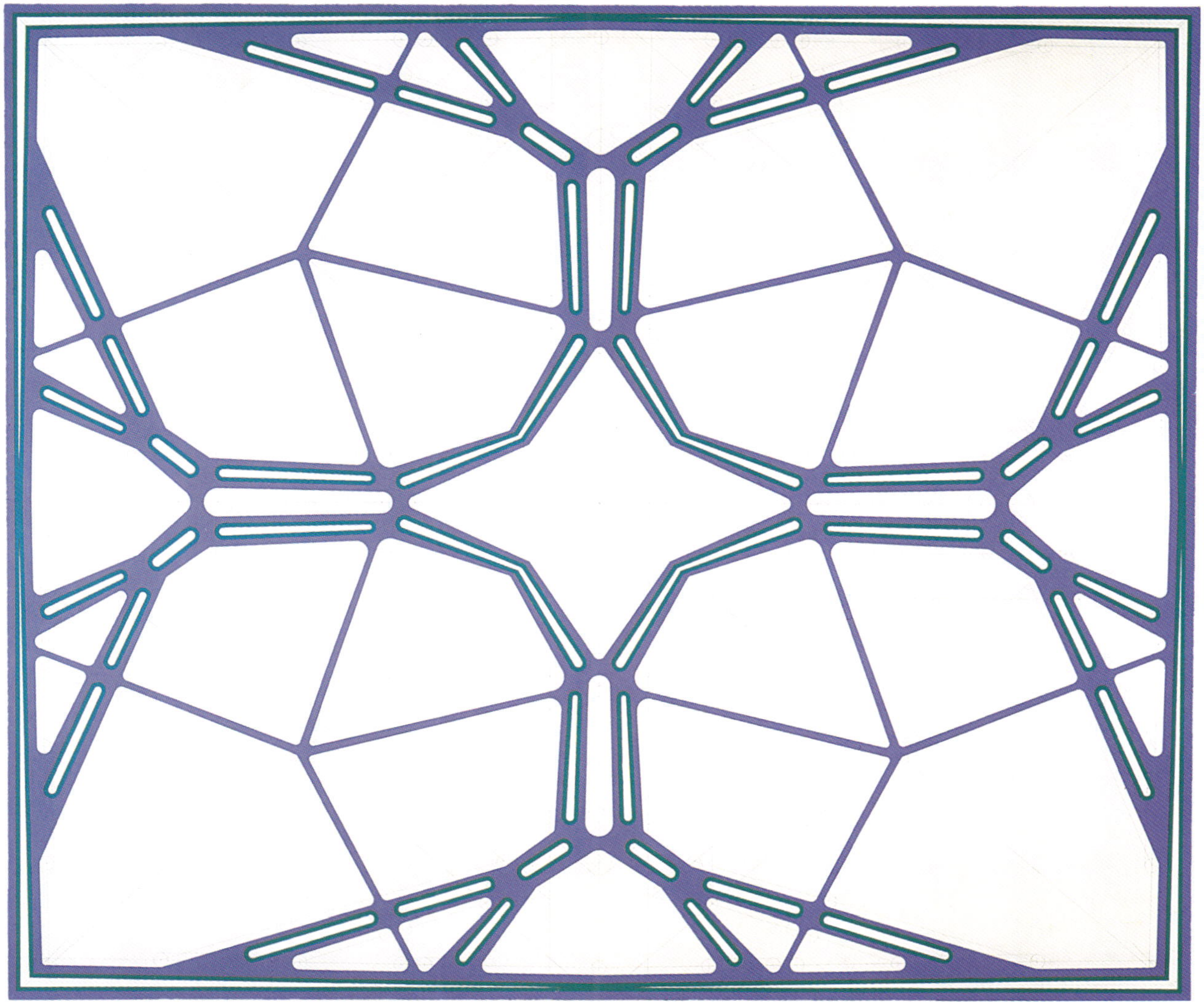

Deviation II

2000

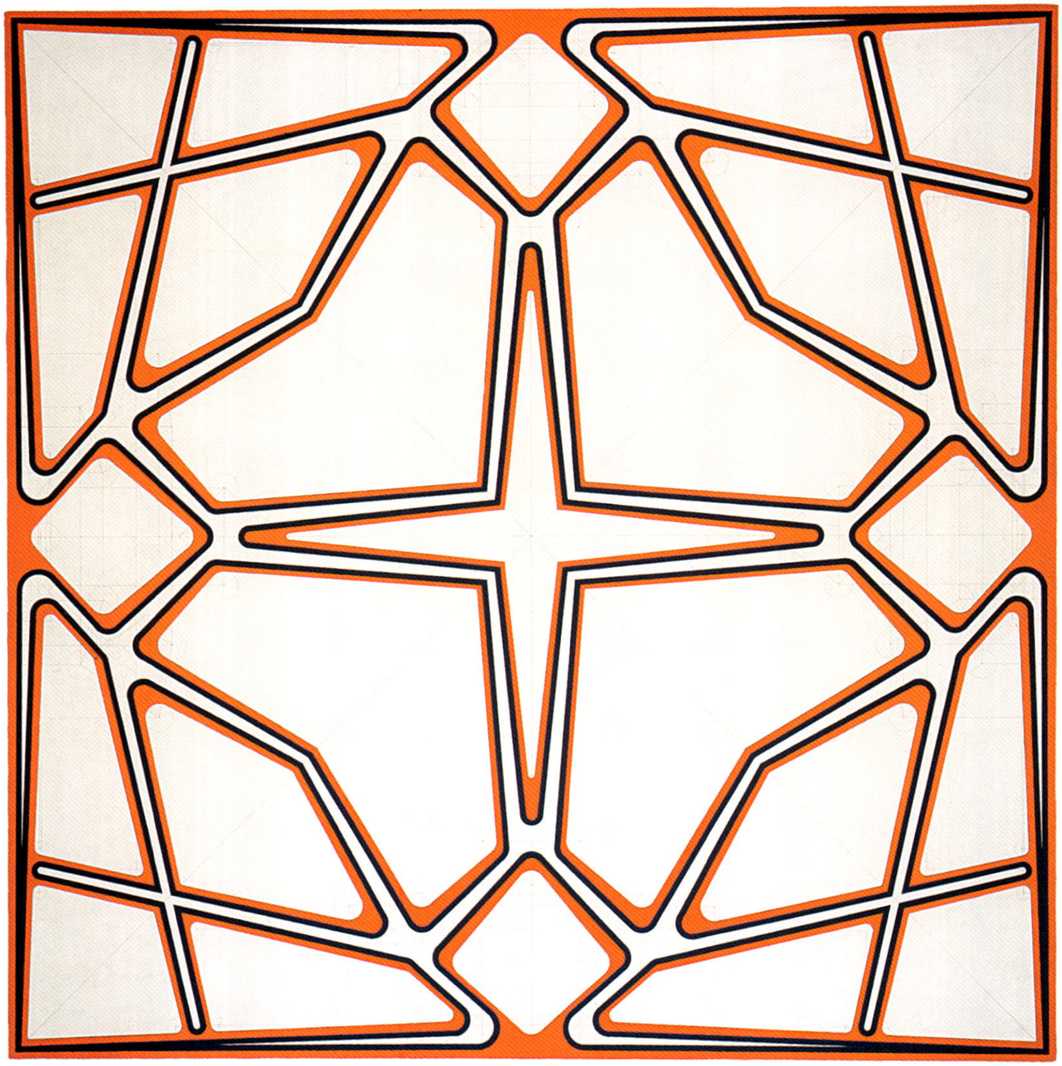

Reversal
2001

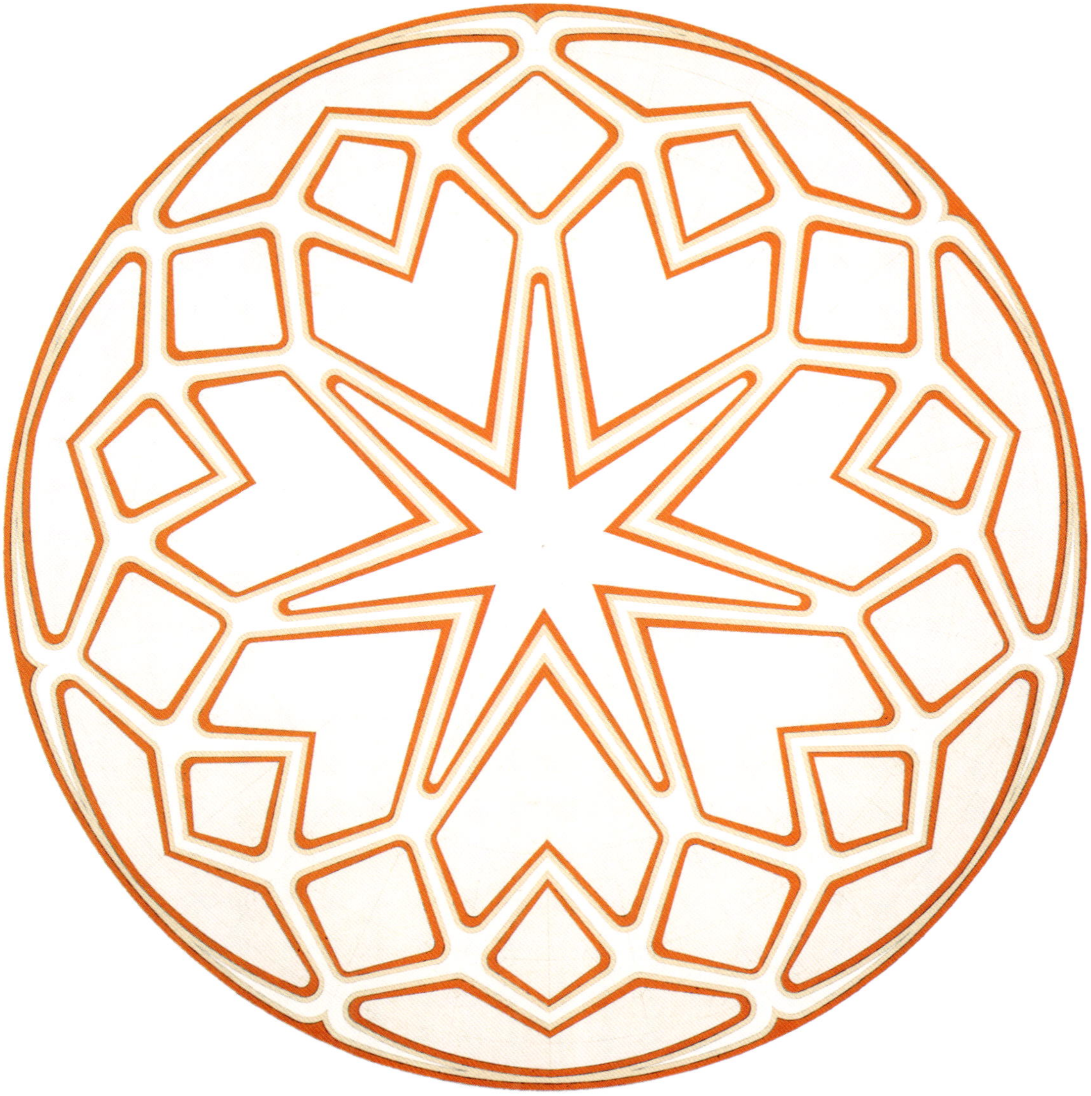

Interlock
2001

[Steven Charles]

I am interested in creating problems. Painting is a vehicle for me to dedicate myself to something I know won't work. Abstract painting is the most confusing dilemma I have encountered; it is this confusion that motivates me. I am not a believer. I am in search of holes and gaps. When I start a painting I don't plan or sketch, I just begin. The beginning could be simple drips, splashes, or paint shot out of a squeeze bottle. Then I work into the initial marks with a process I call targeting. This is where a shape is filled in with a smaller shape, leaving only the outer edge of the first shape showing. This process is repeated until the amount of shape being covered is reduced to the smallest part possible with the selected brush. Each painting begins to generate a logic unique to its own composition. Even though it's obvious that I am making these paintings, the end results always educate me on what I'm doing. The impetus for this work is my optimism, although what I am optimistic about constantly escapes me.

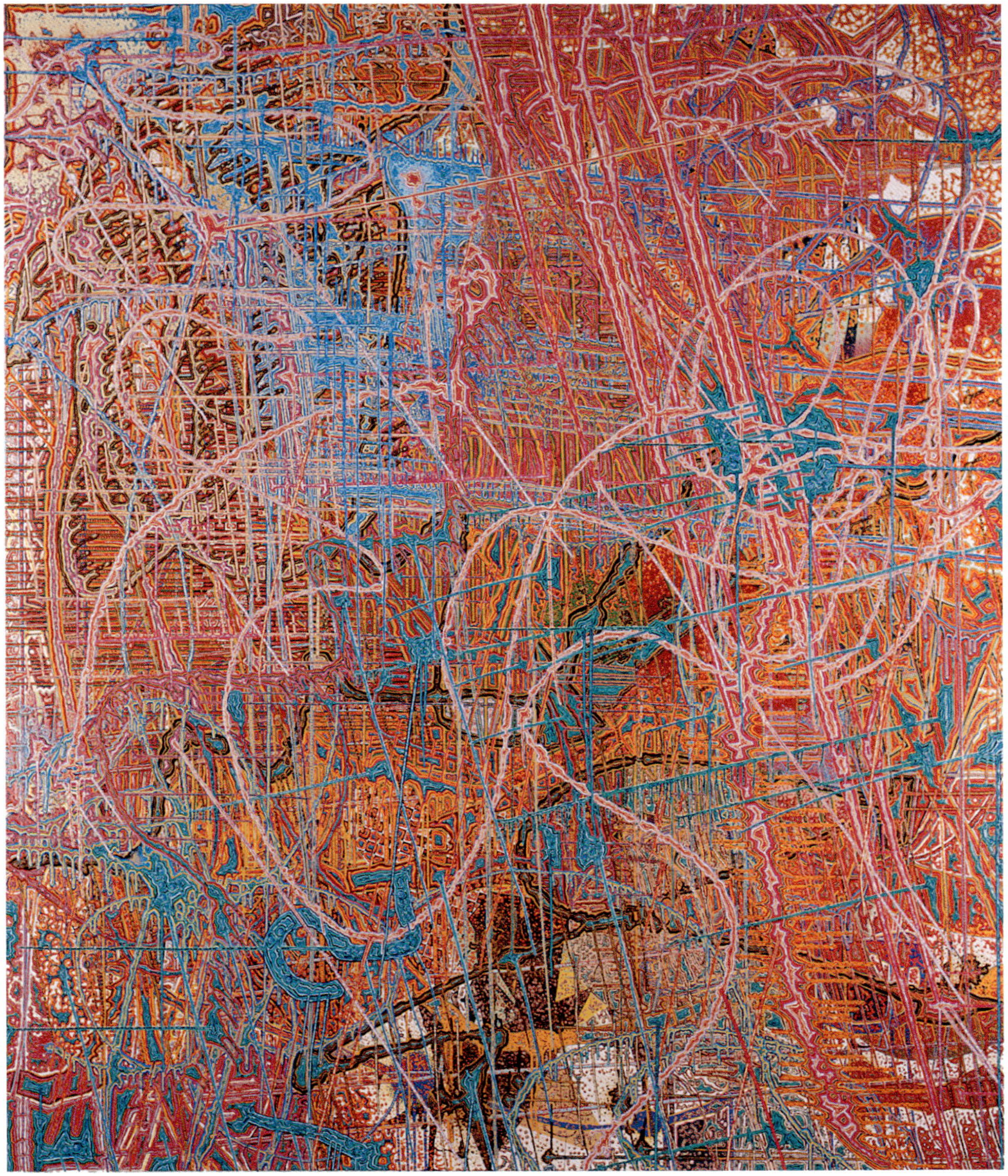

eifoinbysetwin
2000

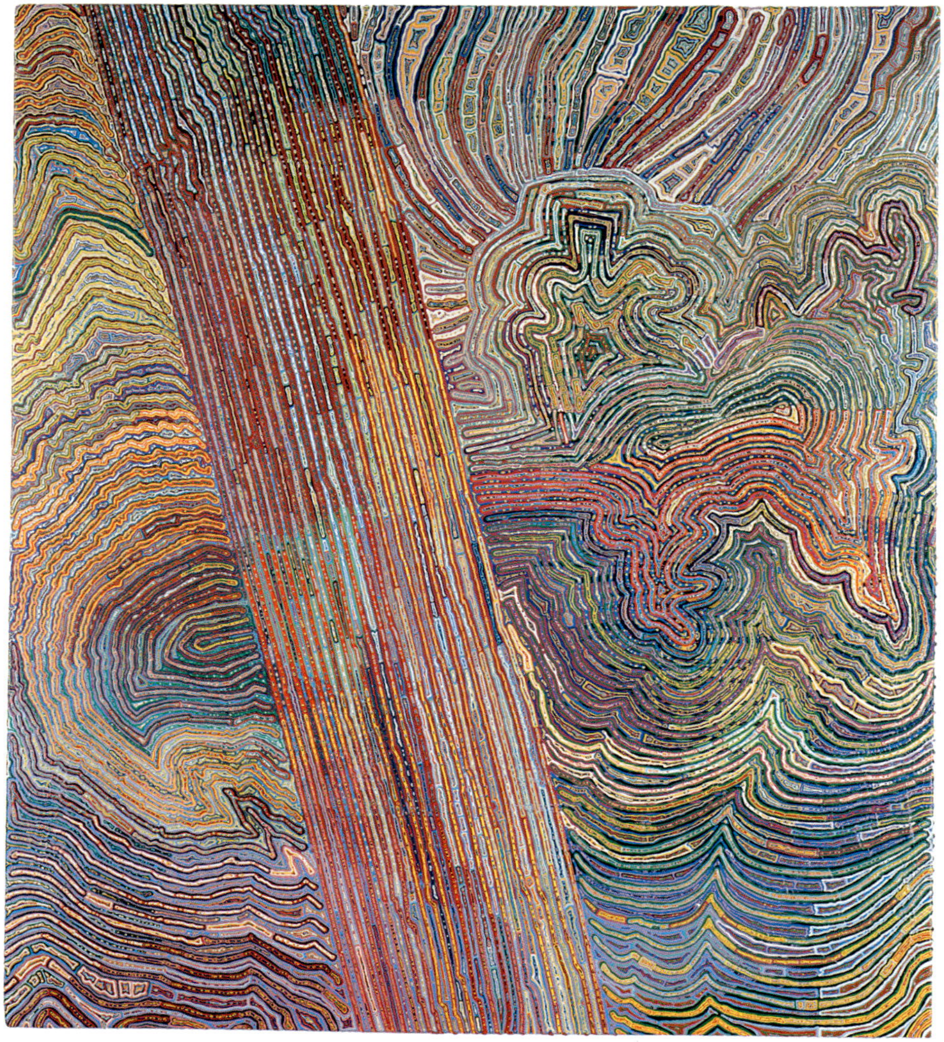

flefpist
2001

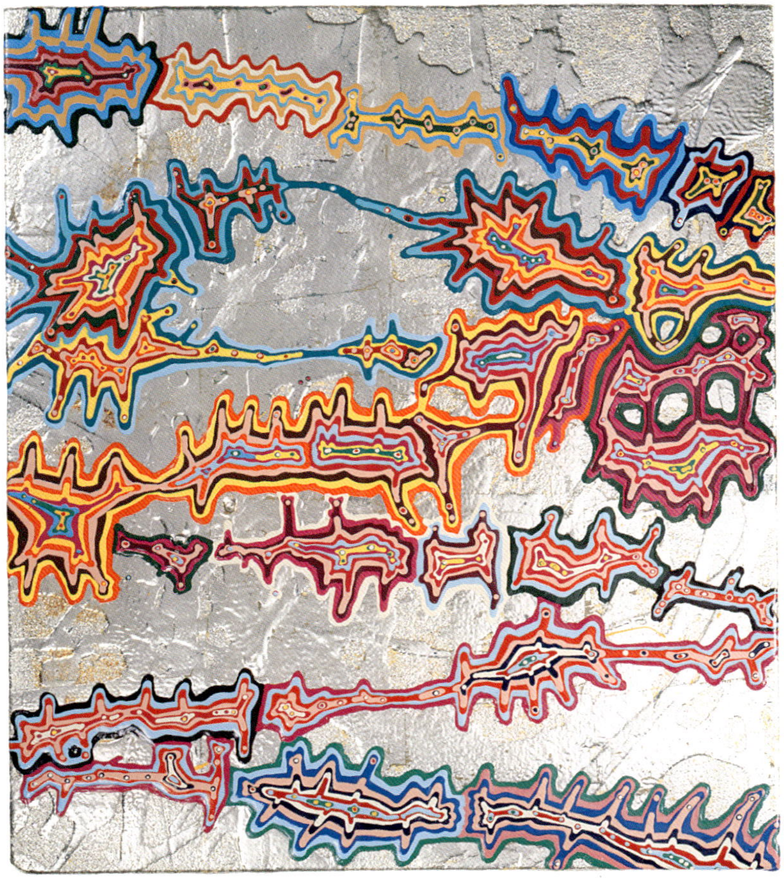

thisonme

2001

[Theresa Chong]

My paintings celebrate color, line, and form. After restraining my color choices for the last ten years to the use of black, white, and grays, I am now surrendering to the seduction of color. Bright, seemingly limitless, and almost fluorescent color, as it appears on the computer screen. And many of the color combinations in my paintings are inspired by color combinations of traditional Korean costumes, which are vibrant and sensuous. Some of my paintings are a mix of layered elements and fragments, and others are about the expansion of freely improvised scribbling.

The use of the computer offers a tremendous amount of freedom and control in image making, enabling me to explore freehand gestures in new ways. The computer has liberated me from the traditional way of working as a painter since I never felt aligned with either Western or Eastern methods of making art.

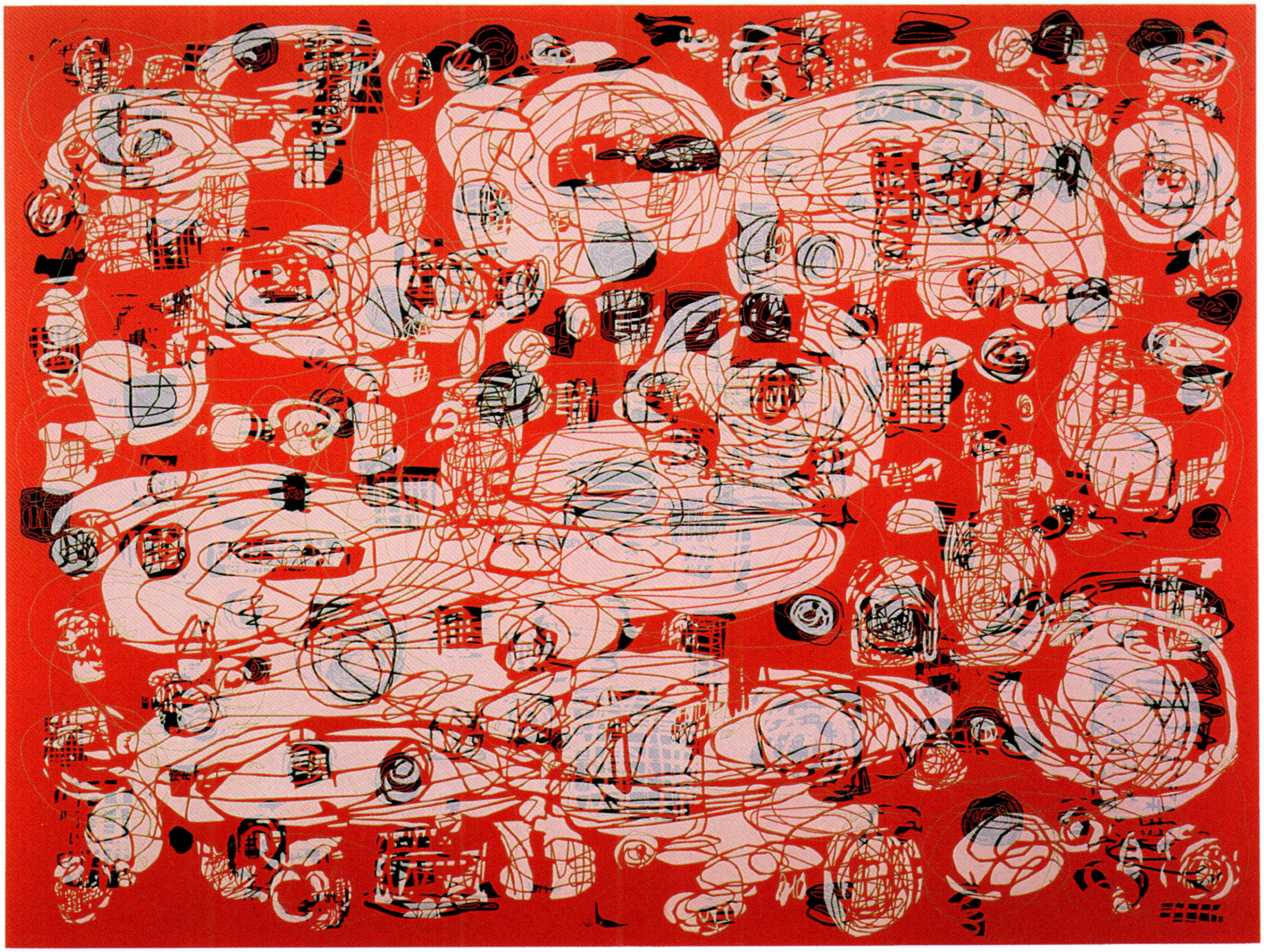

Untitled

2001

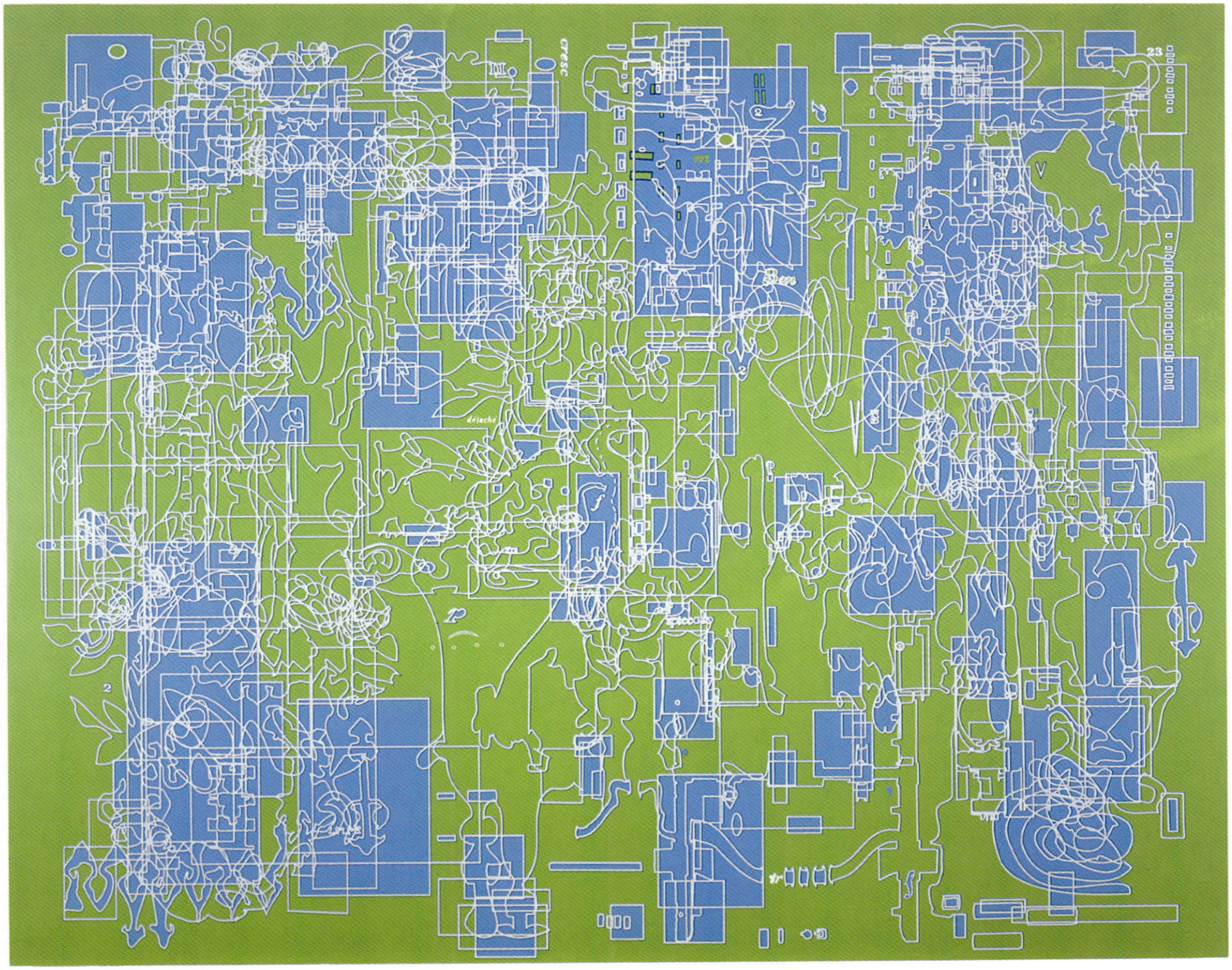

Untitled

2001

[Christopher Francione]

My paintings take shape through the reference to image. Although the work presents itself as abstraction, it is rooted in representation. Through distortion of line and exaggeration, visual elements that were once literal become abstract. I am interested in the space between these opposing elements. Through the process of painting the literal meaning of the original image becomes open-ended, and focus turns to the aesthetic and formal aspects of the piece. It is important for me to keep the elements of the new picture similar to the original, ultimately evoking questions as to the picture's references and history. The images seem to take on their own identity when they venture into the realm of the unrecognizable. Carrying a new definition, they evolve into a painting that is abstract yet strangely familiar. I often trace clippings from comics or cartoons as a starting point for a painting. The line quality of these tracings is an aspect that remains through the painting process and seems to stay potent through the distortion and editing of the original. The comic-book aesthetic of outline and tracing has always been a source of investigation for me. The images seem pure in their mechanical execution and simple elements of solid color and black line. It is this simplicity which allows for easy distortion and redefinition. Ultimately the paintings reside as a new mutated and sometimes ludicrous copy of the original, with residual elements that raise questions as to their content as well as their meaning.

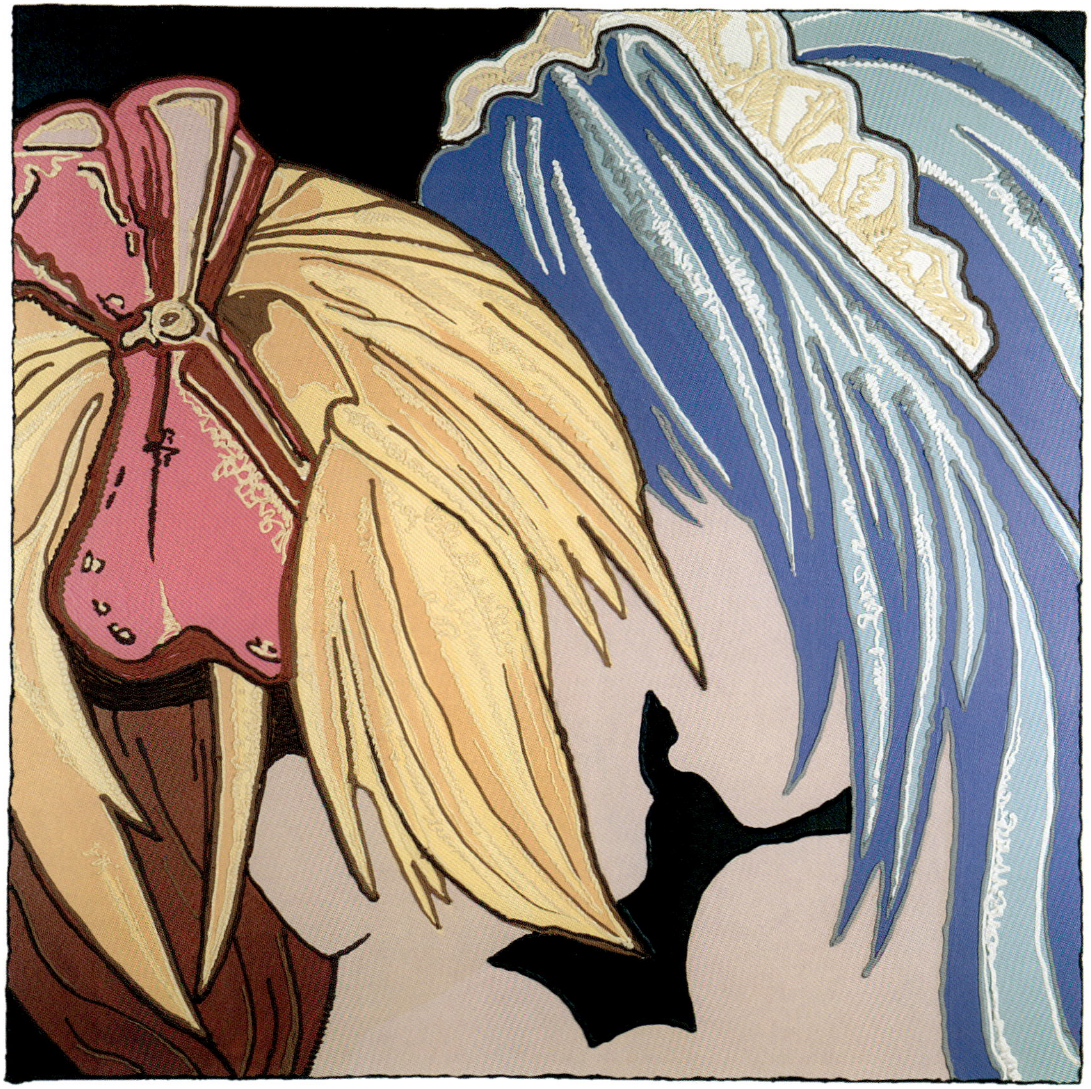

Pink

2001

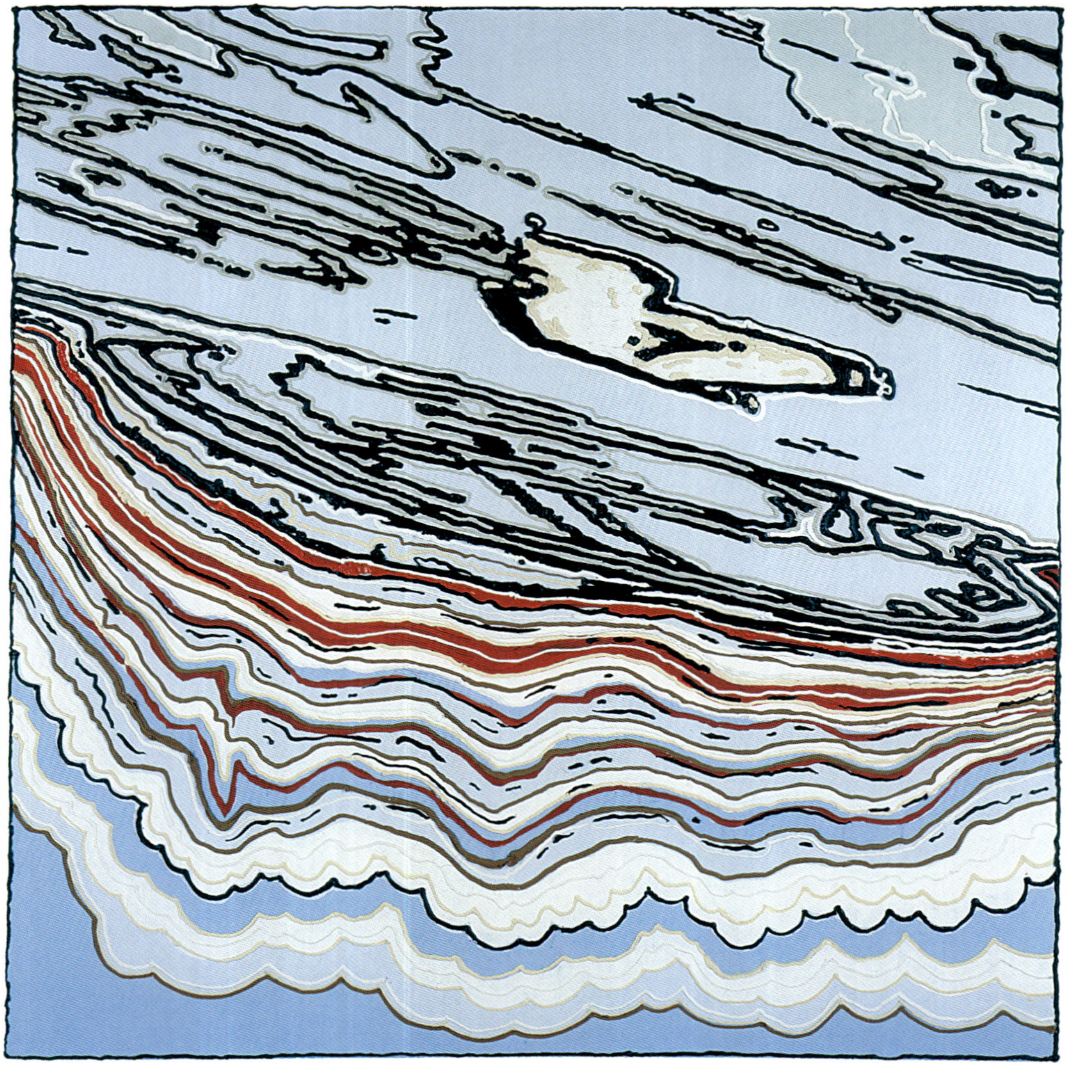

Touchdown

2001

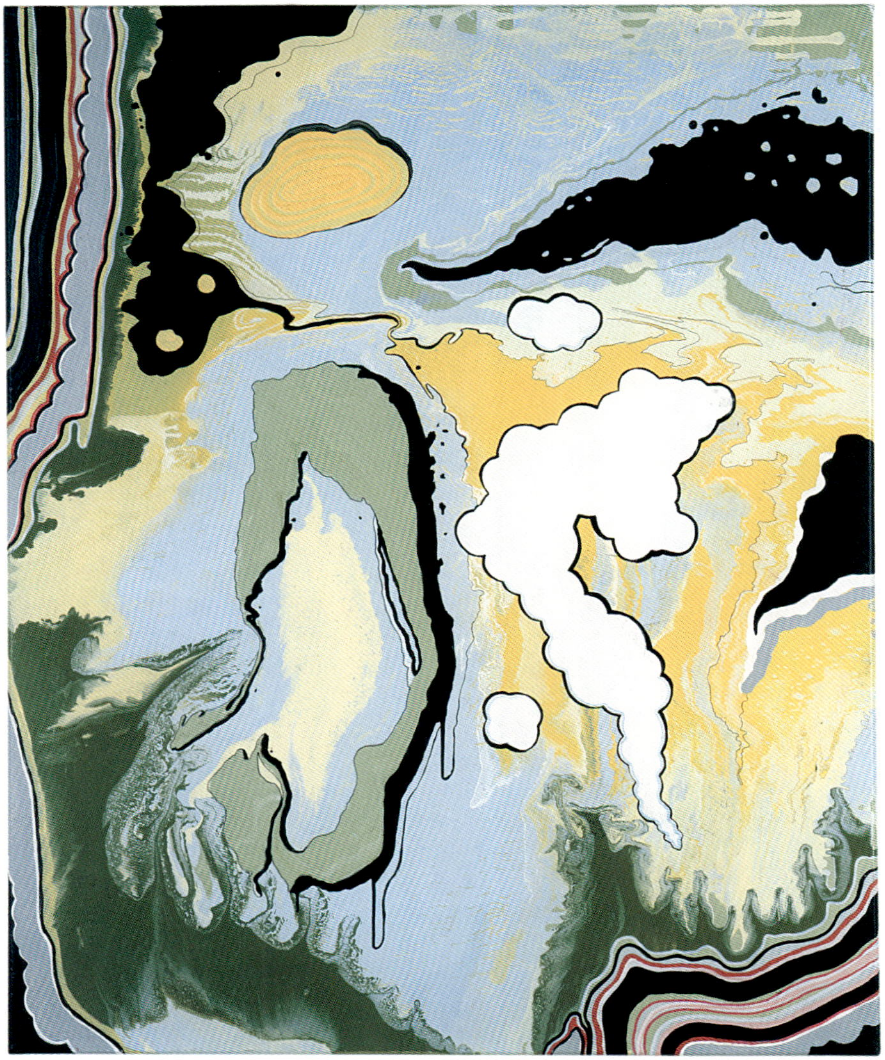

Untitled

2001

[Kathleen Kucka]

In this body of work, acrylic paint is my subject matter. I am working with the "plasticness" of the paint. It can be sanded and poured, it can be cut and reattached. It's physical. There is sensuality in the paint's liquidity. It is a challenge to control. The direct process of pouring paint makes the work spontaneous and personal. As the paint flows over the surfaces of aluminum and Mylar, forces of movement direct the forces of shape and form. The poured marks undulate and flow, join and repel in a dance of space and gesture. The lines flow and collide amongst themselves. The watery substance of these drawings is engaged in a dialogue with notions of control and nature, at times referencing pools of water, fluid mechanics, and atmospheric energies.

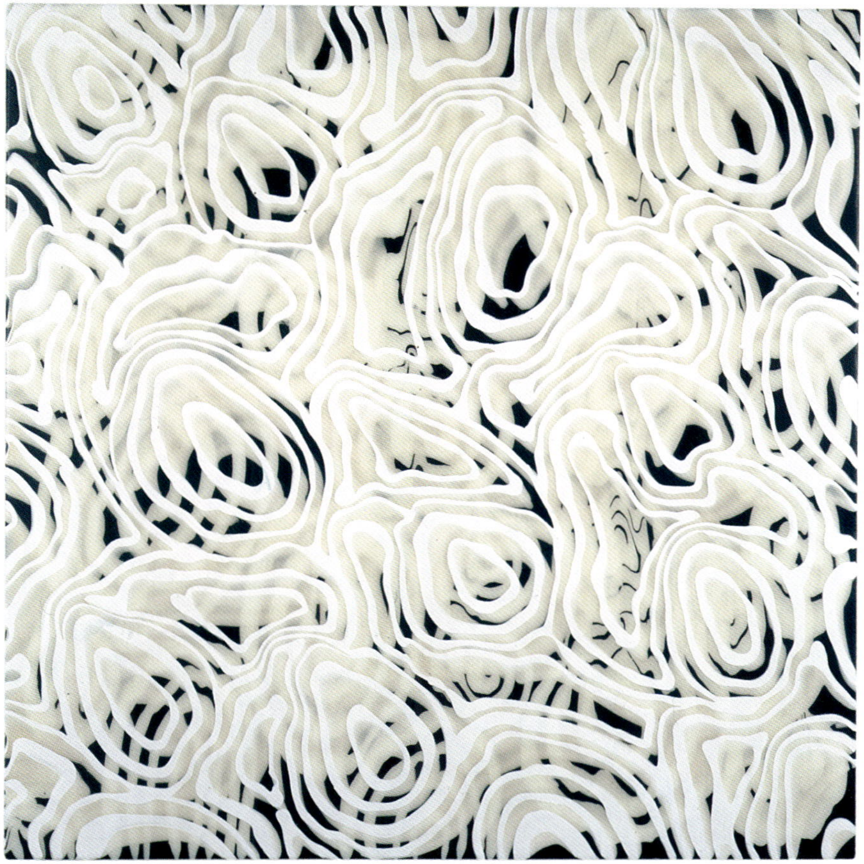

Petite L'une au L'autre

2001

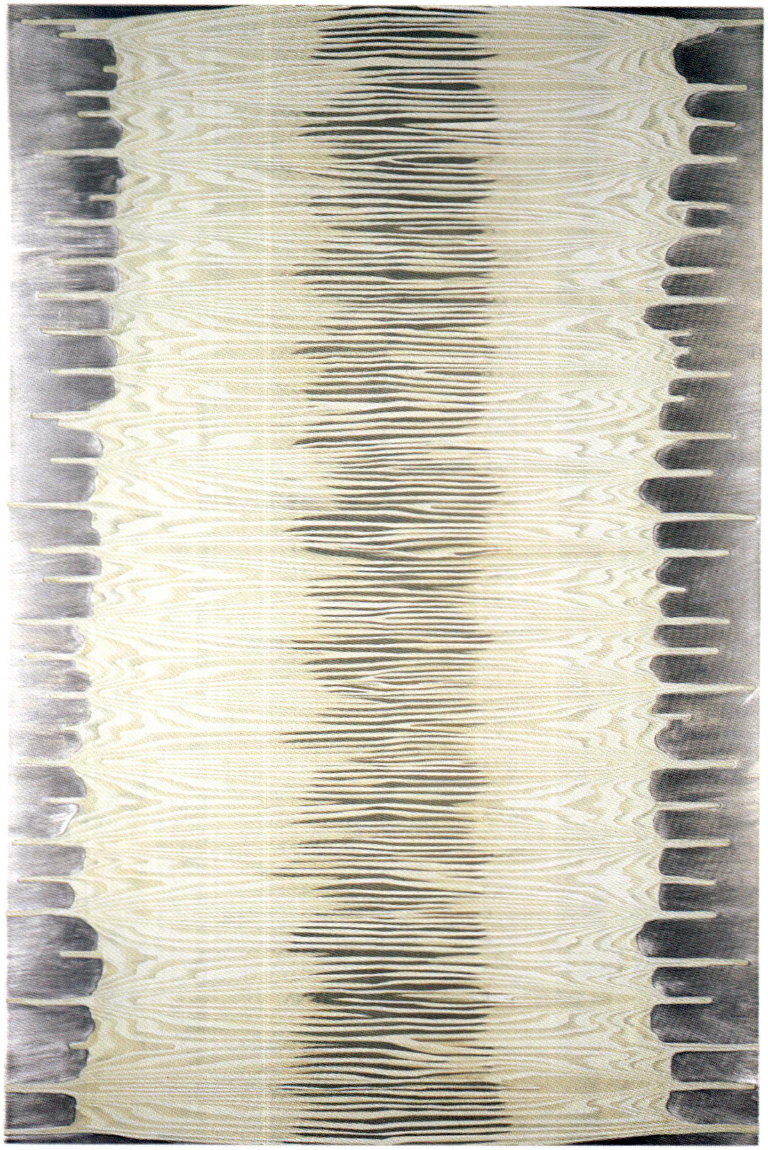

Grip, Grab

2000

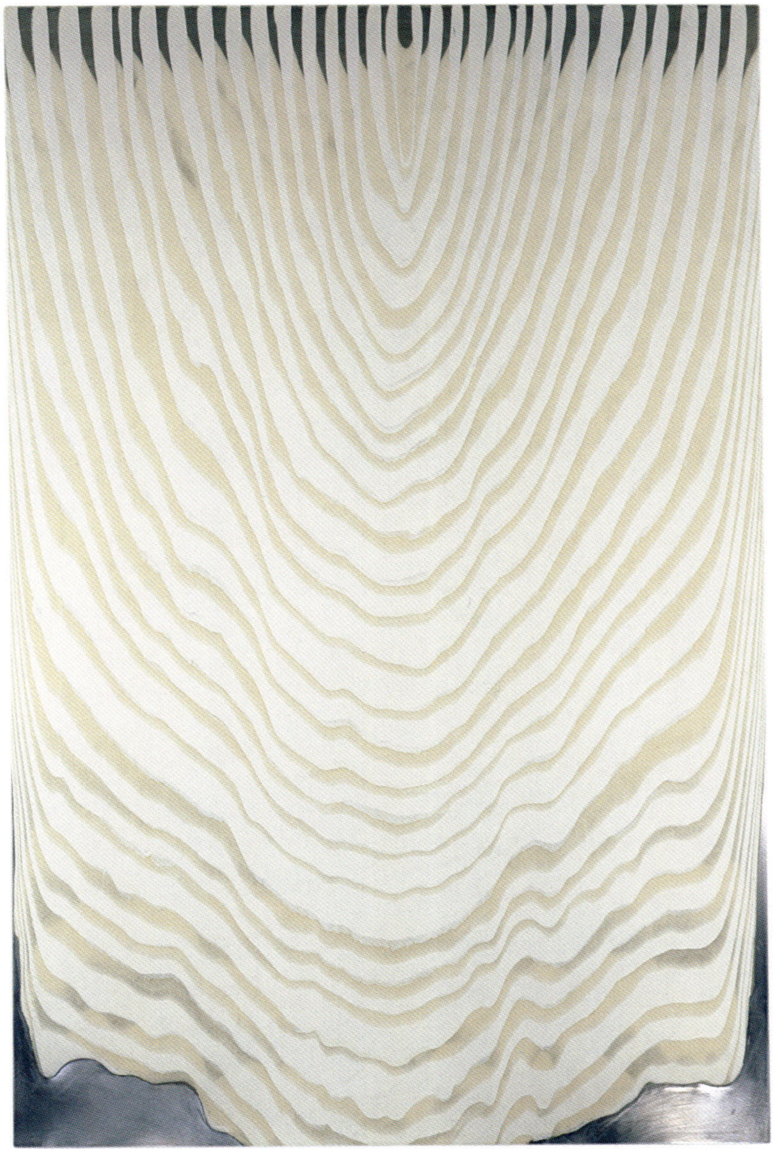

Untitled Fall #2

2000

[Jennifer Riley]

My work sits in the crossroads of lyrical and classic modern abstraction. The structures of these paintings, their off-square format, the internal geometrics, and their relationship to architecture owe their inheritance to modernist and minimalist strategies. Exploration of the material and the immaterial through depictions of flat and illusionistic space is at the heart of my project.

My work aims to extend the poetry of the vivid and the obscure, the immediate and the recollected. This allows me the freedom to explore multiple points of entrance, ranging from the thermal to the musical and the emotional. In each case, my goal is to invite viewer participation through association. Unabashedly recalling the evanescence of sun and moonlight, these paintings strive to evoke an enigmatic tranquility that engages the intuitive mind.

While I make work that expands to include installation, my mental process and the results are firmly rooted in the language and tradition of painting. The images and forms suggest structures analogous to the rural and urban landscape. These paintings of abstract spaces resonate with energy and have echoes of light seen through the curtain of atmosphere. Responses to the built environment are played out in the leaning paintings as well as in the banded conventional paintings. The leaning paintings cast colored shadows against the support wall, lyrically intermingling as shadow illusions. In the banded paintings, carefully orchestrated translucent bands of color diffuse horizontally across smooth and brightly gessoed grounds. The separation of colors and intensity hearkens back to both modern and classic American Hudson River School painting.

The thrill of mystery achieved with basic tools and the colored medium of paint deliberately arranged by hand continue to focus in my mind, efforts, and imagination.

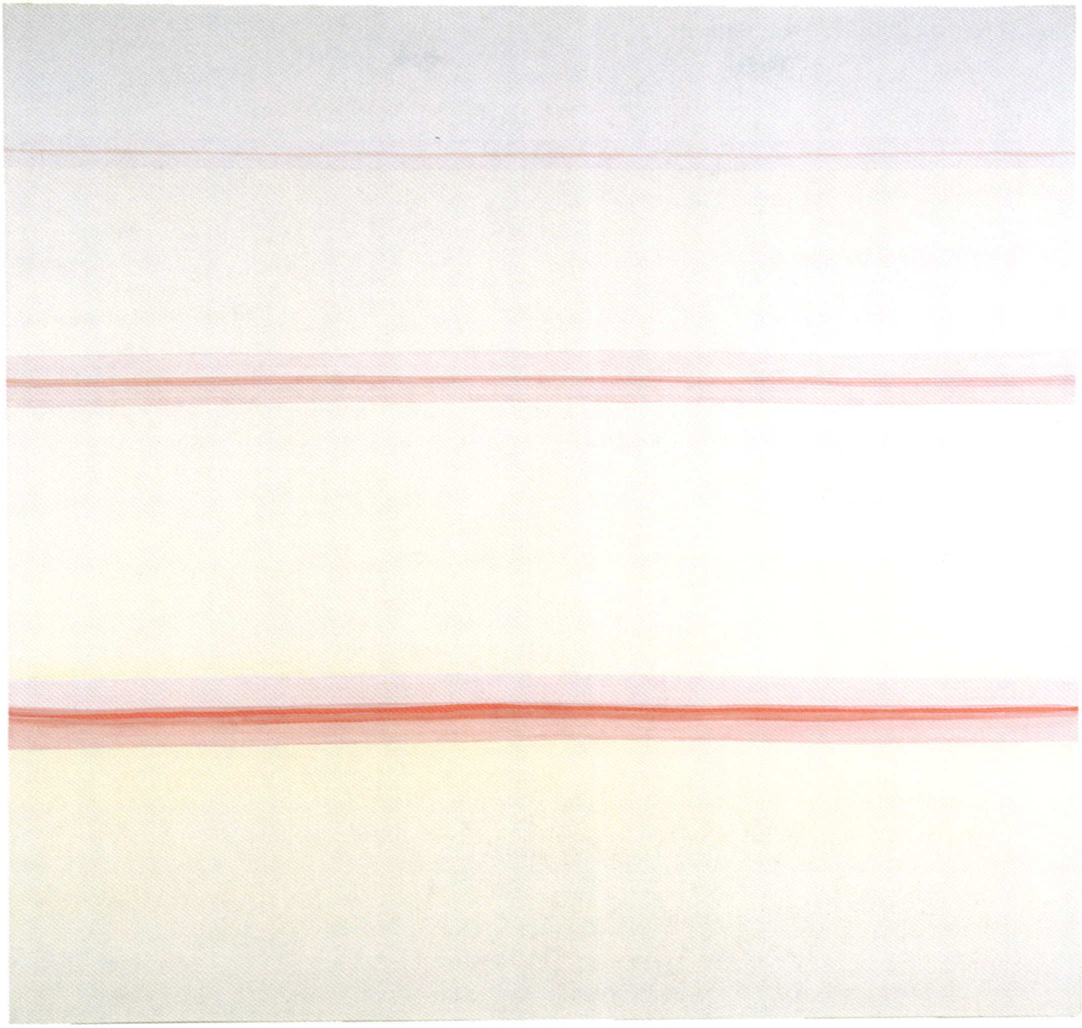

New Rules for Romance
2000

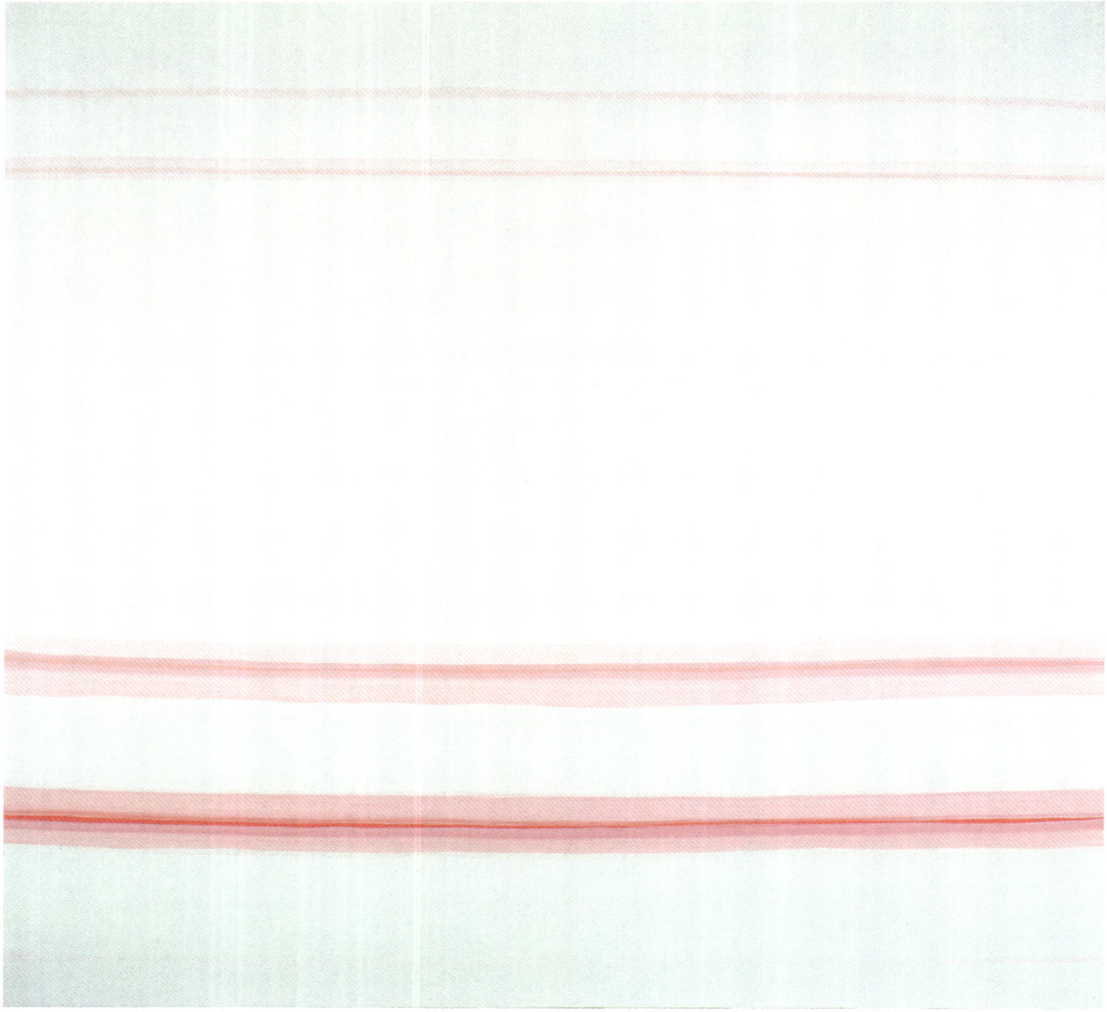

Borrowed Kisses

2000

Biological Flutter
2001

[Lisa Stefanelli]

Many of my paintings pay homage to characters, places, and movements referred to in both contemporary life and classical mythology. (By this I mean architecture and popular cultural aesthetics and commercial imagery, for instance, Americana.) Being an incurable romantic, I am overly sentimental about these things, and their demise. One of my paintings is titled *Grass Widow*, which is a reference to an obscure character in Sholokhov's novel *And Quiet Flows the Don*. There are also paintings titled *Kressman's Farm* and *Stout's Valley*. This valley and farm no longer exist; they are currently being replaced by housing developments. My paintings represent the places and people which I recognize as being so valuable to our understanding of our cultural vision yet are generally overlooked and taken for granted. My paintings pay homage to these unsung characters of our mythology: from the characters of the classics to the old barns crumbling in the farming valleys of the landscape in which I grew up.

As a painter, I am interested in the audience who doesn't stop to read the classics...those who not only don't stop to read the books, but who also don't notice the architecture or the open fields, or the urban sprawl, or the old Chevrolets. The audience I'm interested in are those who happily replace the old with the new. The "McMansions" that dot the valleys of rural America are full of occupants who seemingly never bother to notice. I am hopeful that the person who doesn't always bother to notice most things will take the time to "look back" at my paintings, and somehow find something familiar. I imagine that this is why they are beautiful. Beauty can be very disarming.

If you are familiar with my work you will know that I was a nationally competitive ice skater, and yes, this simple fact did and does play a very significant role in the vocabulary I use to make paintings. I have an innate understanding of movement in physical space...and, most likely, the reason I use lines and twists and turns in my paintings is because I have succumbed to such a complete understanding of this movement. My paintings are not about landing a successful double loop or triple lutz. But in a way, the ice-skating "gene" is very appropriate in my endeavors as a painter. After all is said and done, when you find yourself flipping through the channels, how can you resist stopping to watch the figure skaters, even if just for a moment?

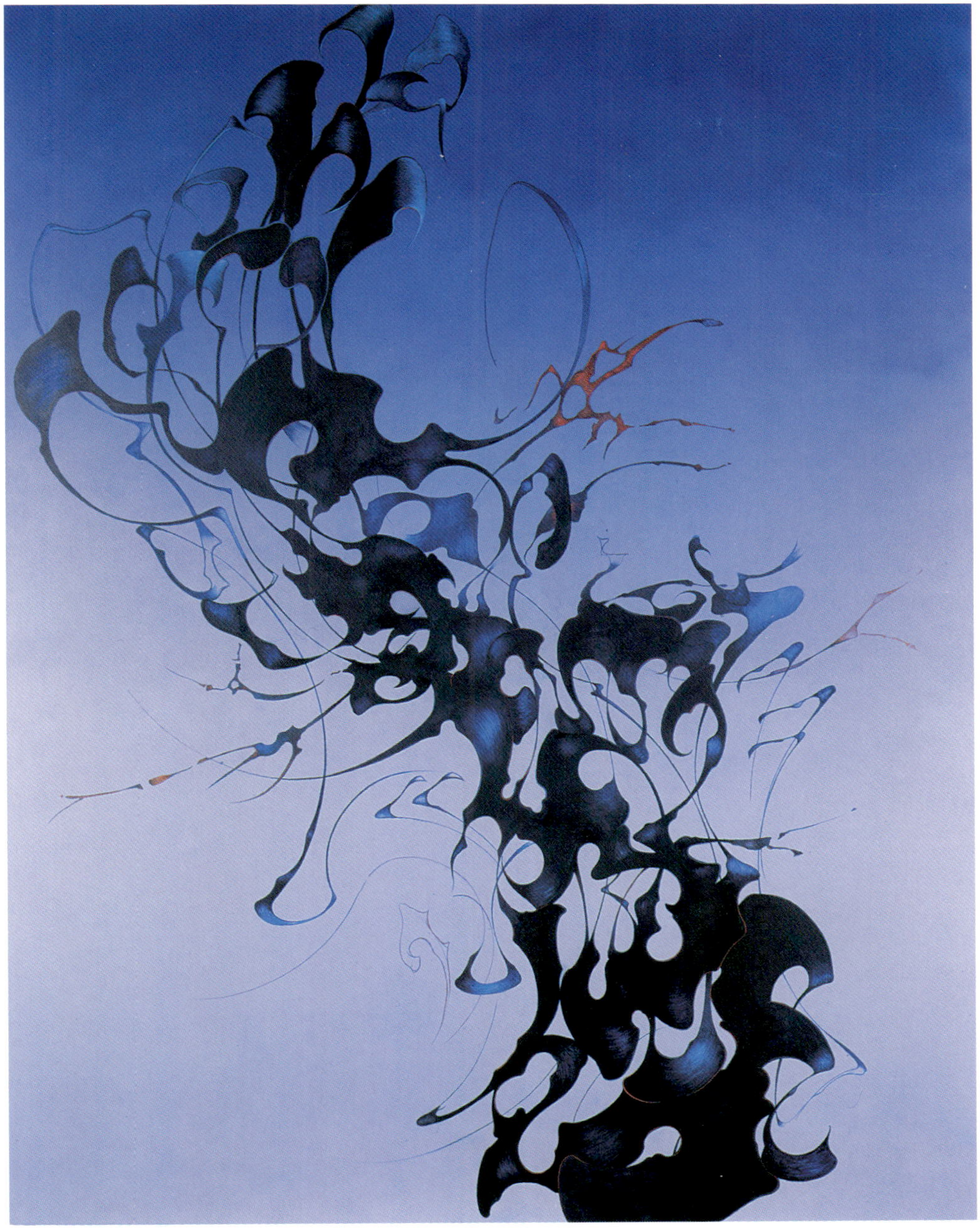

Thornfield (The Horse Chestnut at Thornfield)
2001

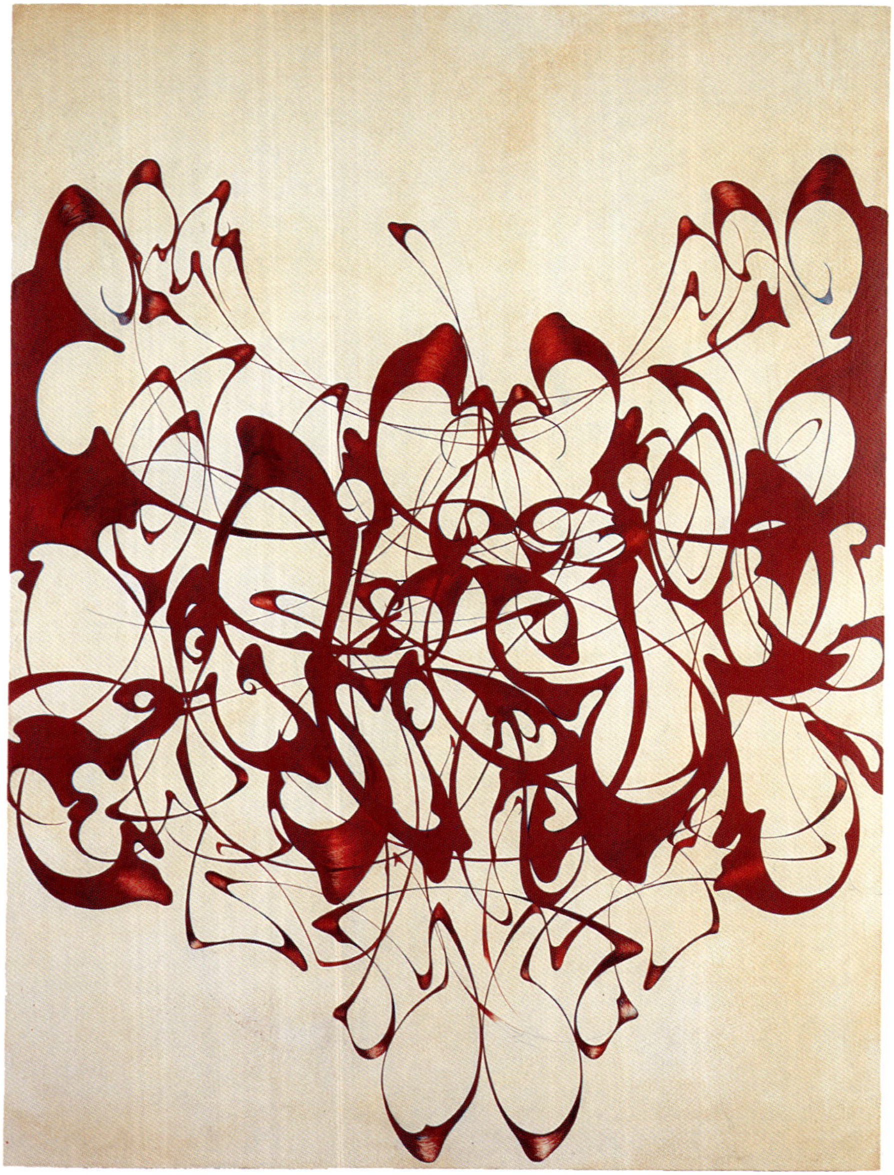

Twisted Sister

2000-01

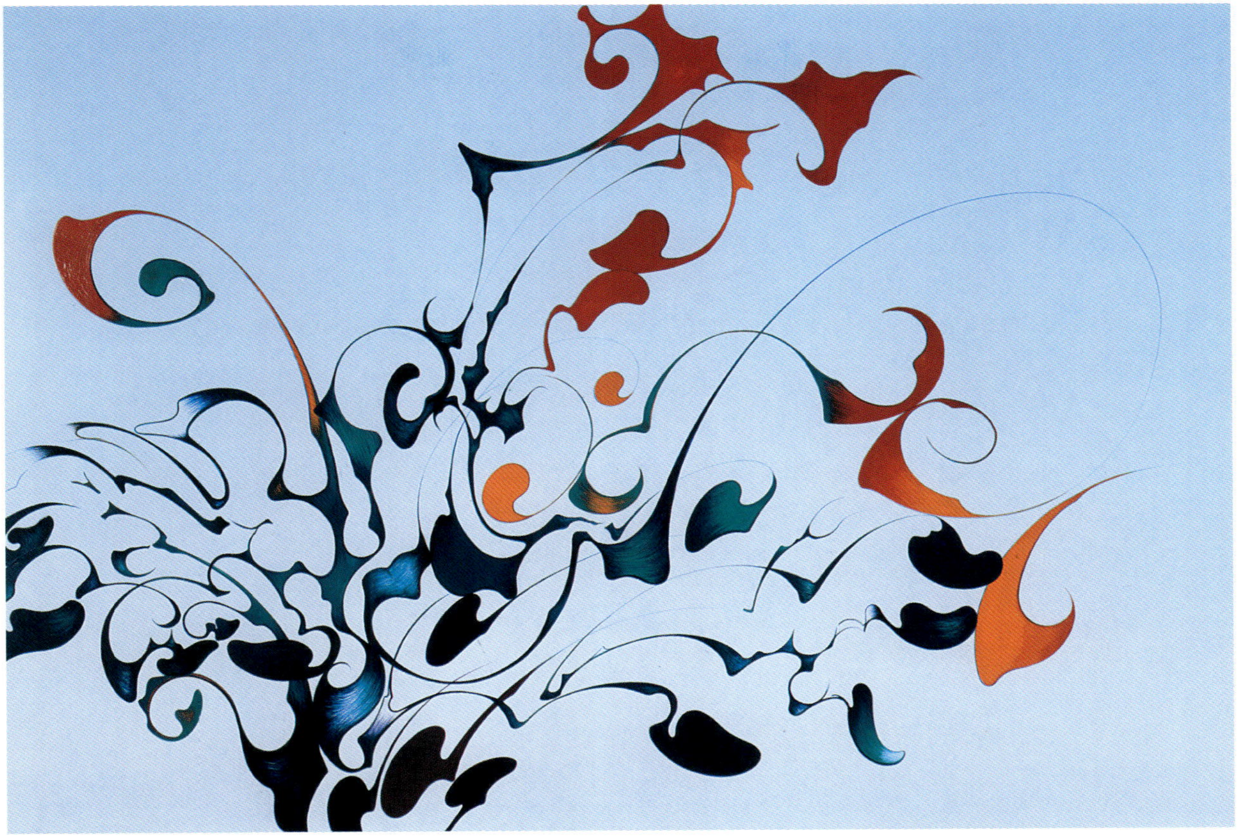

The Grass Widow
2001

[Hiroshi Tachibana]

Since I was 21 years old, I have been looking for presence of being, which is possible but difficult to explain as mind space, or space attached to the mind. At that time I actually had a horrible traffic accident and expected to die at any moment. While unconscious, I had a very strange experience that I can only call a vision of enlightenment. Though a transient image, I strongly remember what I felt. I could feel my existence in this great moment of immersive space. The temperature was perfect...not too warm or cold. I recall unexplained, colorful white light that was specifically white, but I felt every single color simultaneously as well. The atmosphere was relaxed and peaceful, but I had moderate tension. The air was gentle, and not too light or heavy. I never felt like this before. This experience is symbolic of the momentum of presence because those memories woke my mind and made me realize what I want out of life. Since then I have looked forward to finding a similar space with such presence. It is difficult to find that place in life because it is immaterial, abstract, and imaginative. I believe that space is everywhere but is subtle, hidden, and shy. Distracted by daily life, we miss many things and do not notice others. Life deserves careful attention and a clear mind.

In my painting, I am interested in such attention that is made by two ideas simultaneously like macro and micro, simple and complex, background and foreground, space and flatness, connection and disconnection, mental and physical. Those dualities never incorporate each other well, but can open the space in our minds to awaken the consciousness. These difficult relationships give us a different perception of the senses and create a broader view of mind. This is the space between my mind and reality. Such unexplained space is the place of "being present," which is difficult to describe. Attention, carefulness, contradiction, and conflict make holes or windows through which we can experience existence. This is my plug to the real world. My paintings are proof of presence and visualize a space where I can breathe and awaken.

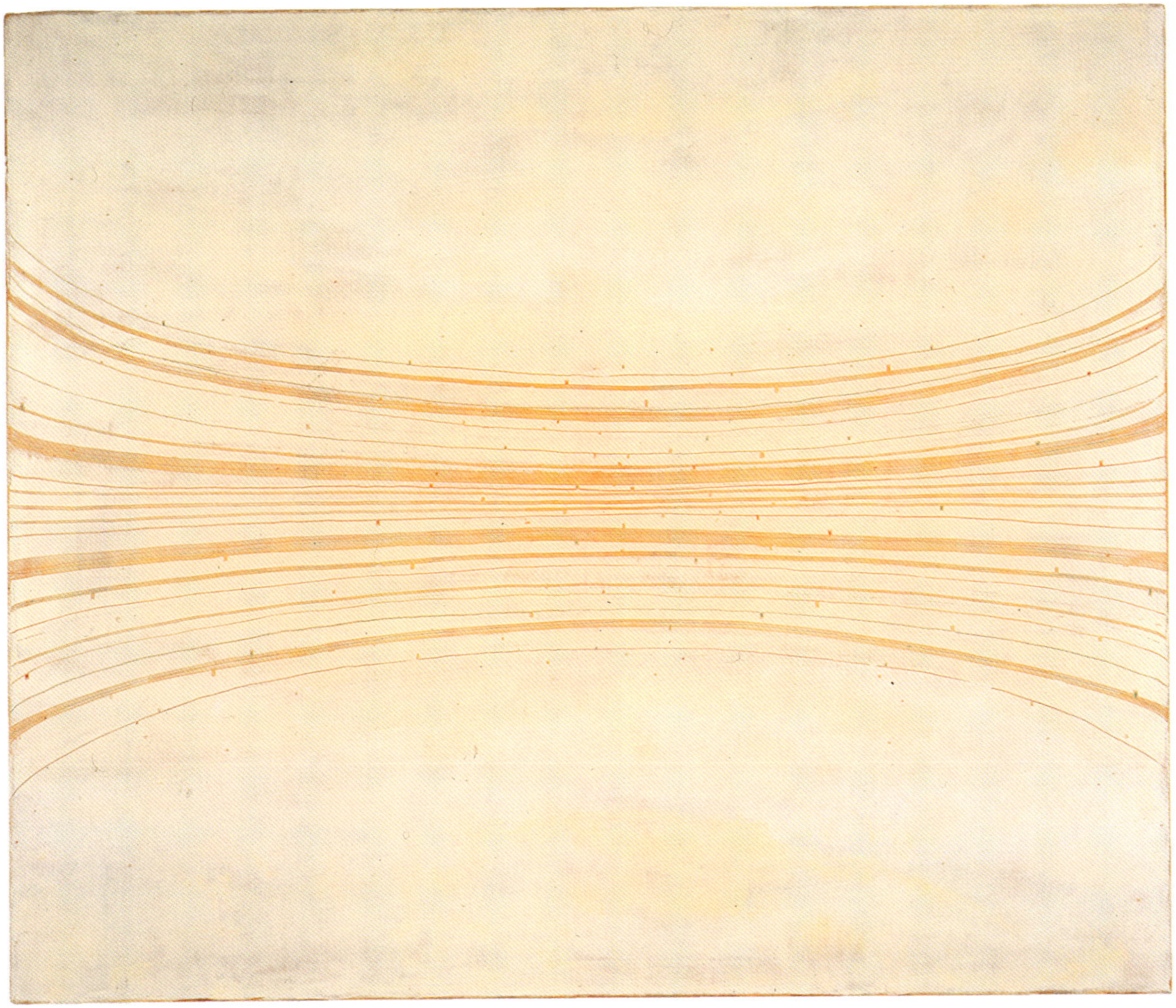

Monster of the Room
2001

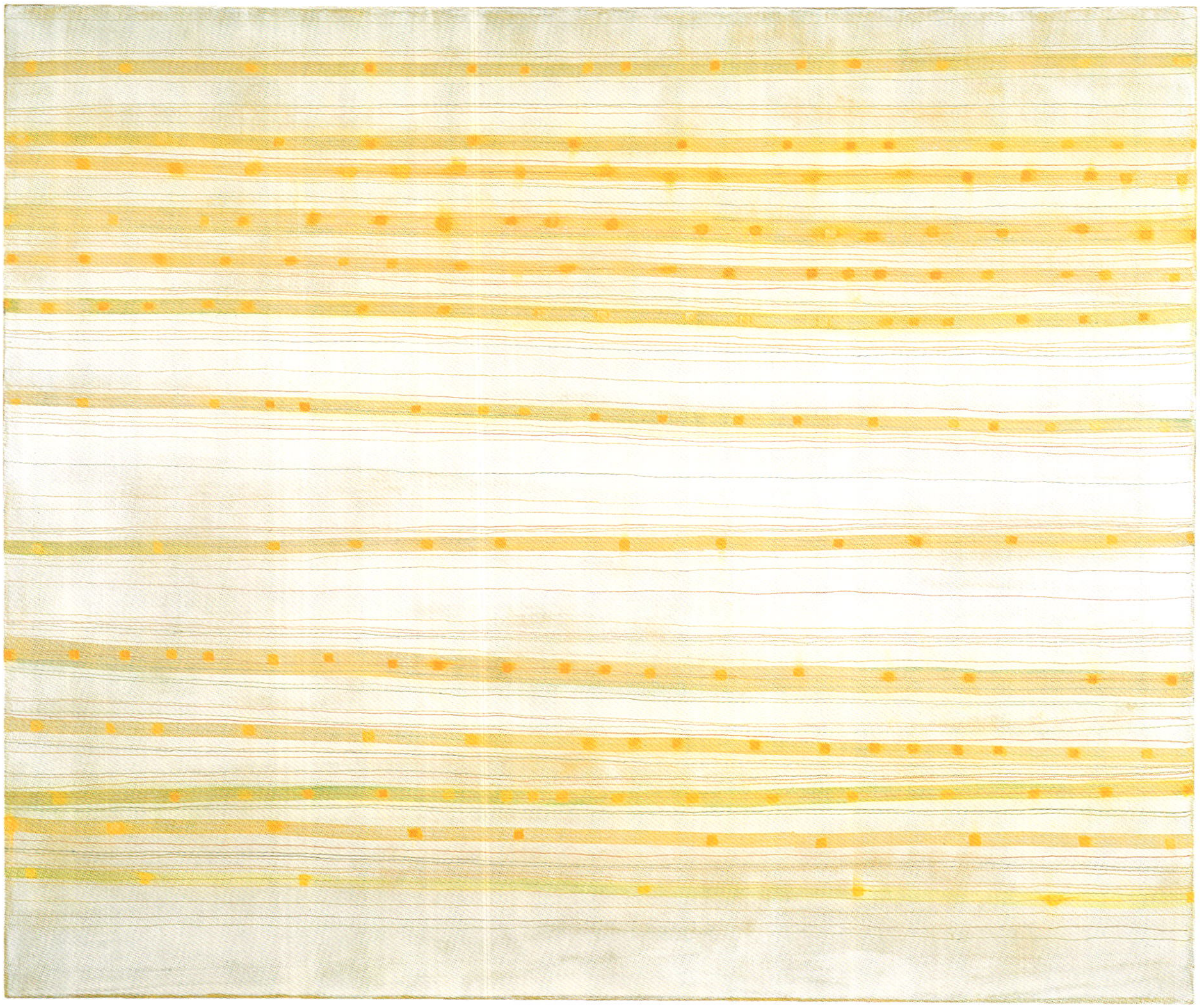

Layer of Joke
2001

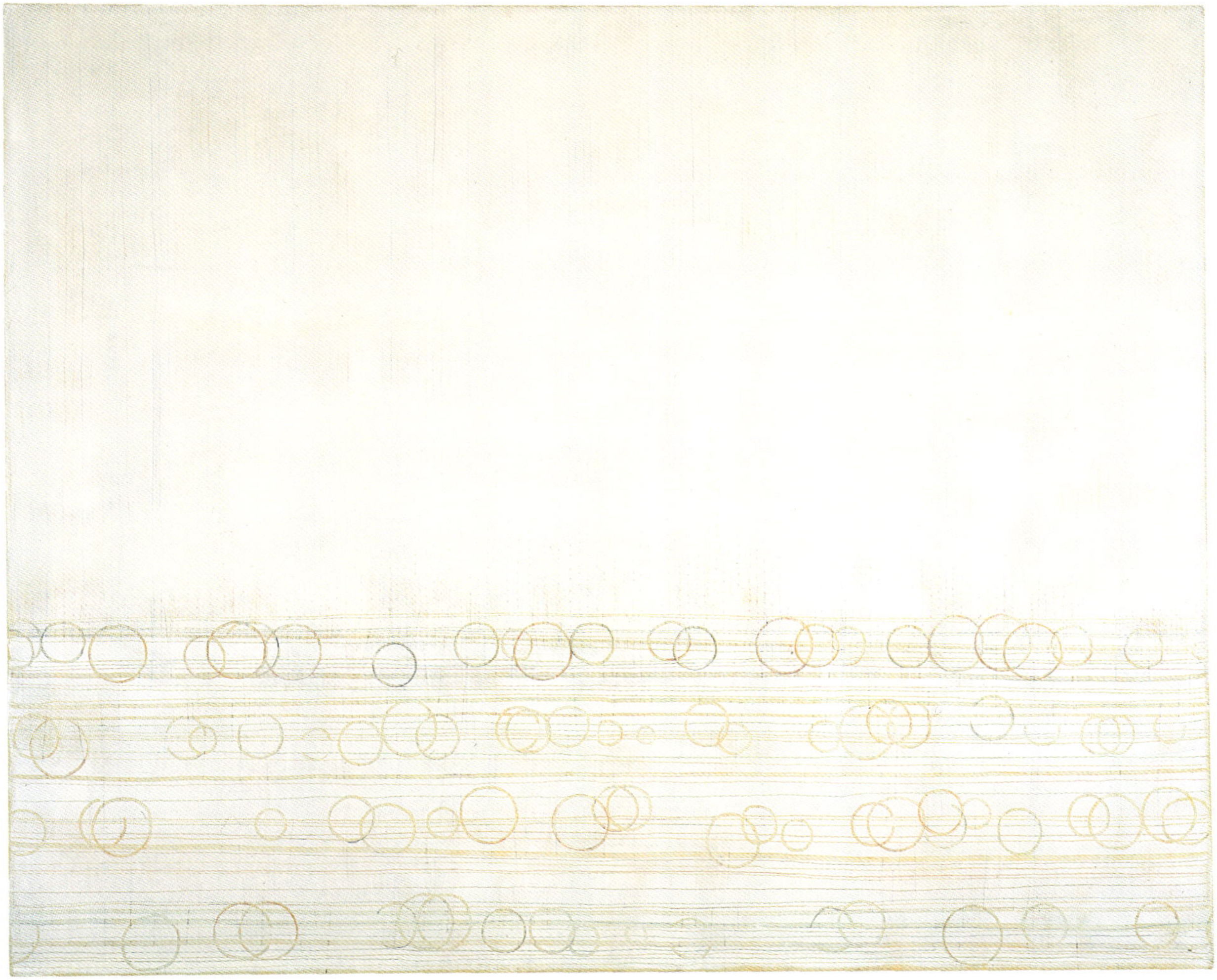

Route 209

2001

[Ana Vilarrasa]

I like the surprise of a gentle contradiction.

I use geometry to question the idea of opposites: masculine versus feminine, abstract v. figurative, rational v. intuitive, visually spare v. visually luscious. My work attempts to reconcile conditions that may, at first, appear contradictory.

But I am also very interested in the works' physical presence: their surfaces, the way their colors may cast a reflection on the wall, how the works are hung, and how their "backs" touch the wall surface.

These elements conspire to give insight into the fragility of geometry. Here is the "lightness" of a pregnant painting, a square façade that may reveal curvaceous dimensions, and a "good, solid argument" with its corners bitten off! I hope to share my skepticism with the viewer and add a pinch of humor!

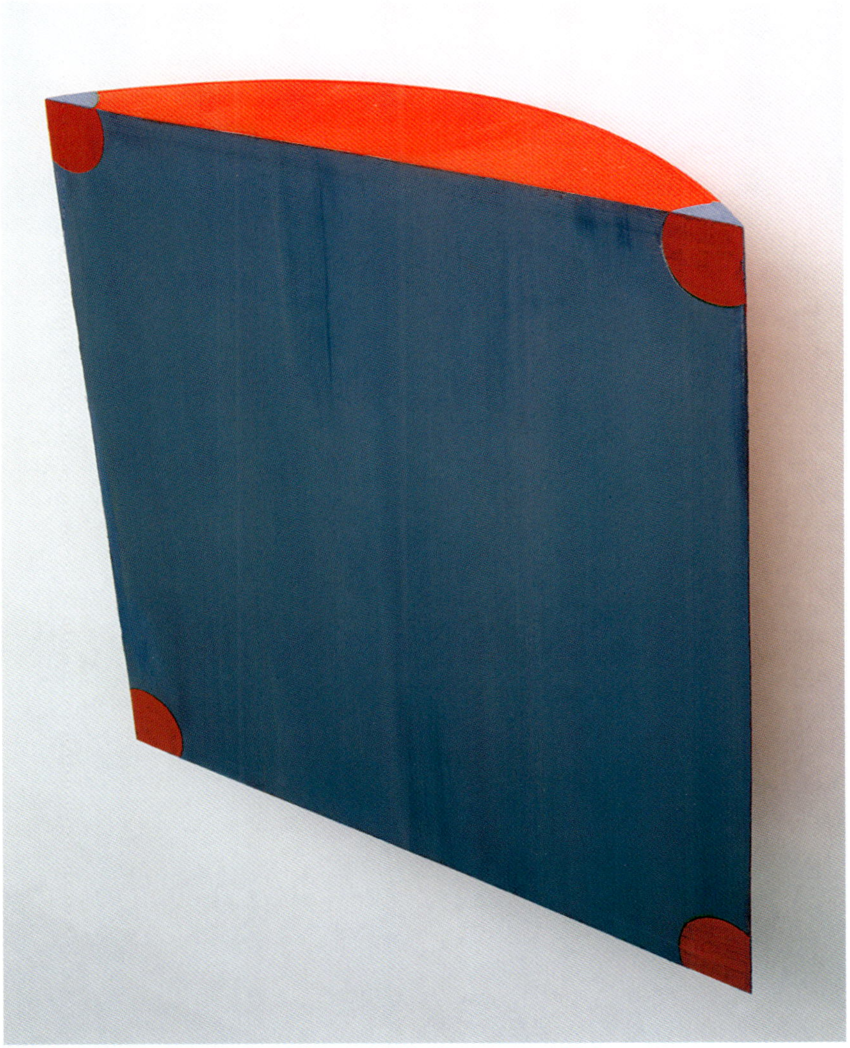

Comic Reason 3
1999

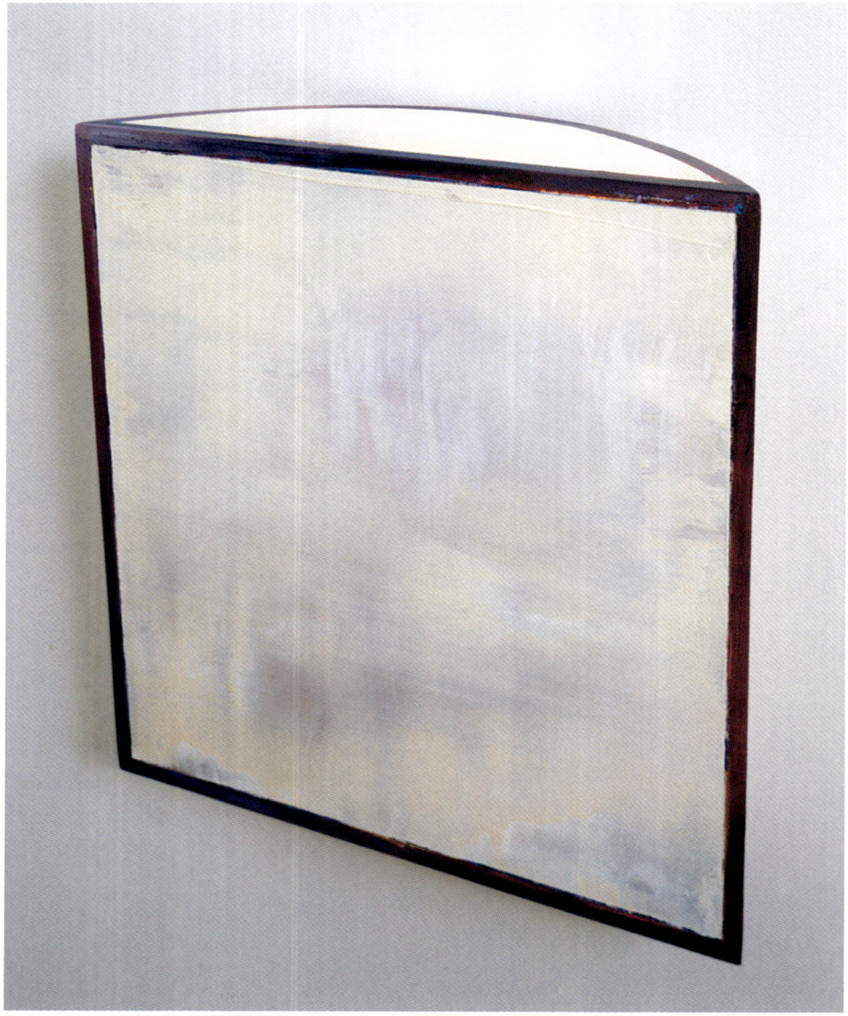

White & Purple Edge
2000

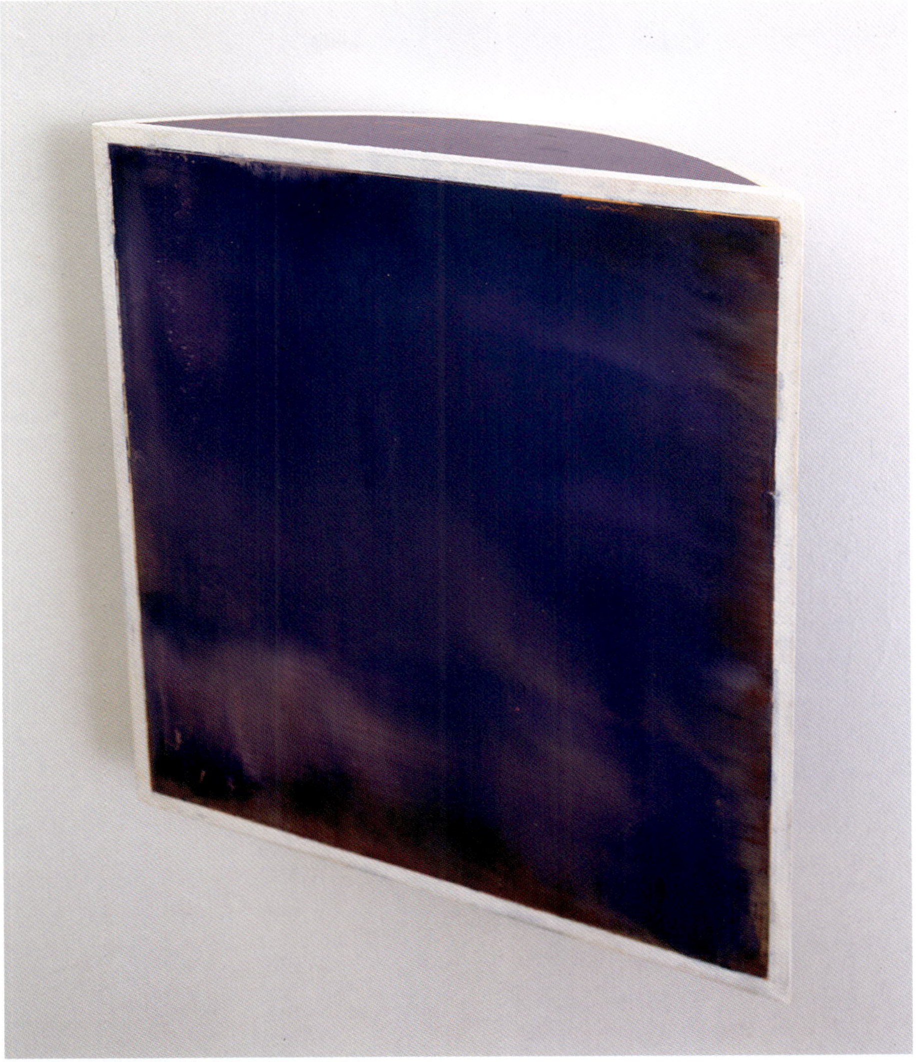

Purple & White Edge
2000

Artists' Selected Biographies

Walter Biggs

Lives in New York, NY

Born

1964 Manhassett, NY

Education

1990 MFA, School of Visual Arts, New York, NY

1986 AB, Hamilton College, Clinton, NY

Selected Exhibitions

2002 *Young + Brash + Abstract*, Anderson Gallery, Virginia Commonwealth University, Richmond, curated by John Yau

2001 *The Armory Show 2001*, Gian Enzo Sperone/exhibitor, New York, NY

Hamilton Makes Art, Ian Peck Fine Paintings, New York, NY

FIAC, Gian Enzo Sperone-Rome/exhibitor, Paris

2000 *Deep Field Painting*, The Bertha and Karl Leubsdorf Art Gallery at Hunter College, New York, NY curated by Michael Brennan

Arte Americana; Ultimo Decennio, Museo d'Arte della Citta di Ravenna, Ravenna

1999 *Walter Biggs: Paintings and Works on Paper*, Sperone Westwater at Bulgari Corporation of America, New York, NY

Walter Biggs, Milleventi, Milan

Then and Now, The Work Space, New York, NY

Group Show, Sperone Westwater, New York, NY

FIAC, Sperone Westwater/exhibitor, Paris

Selected Bibliography

Hamilton Makes Art, exhibition catalogue, Ian Peck Fine Paintings, NY, 2001. Foreword by William Sazillo.

Gualdi, Stefano. *tema celeste contemporary art* 81 (July-September 2000), p. 85. Review of *Arte Americana, Ultimo Decennio.*

Arte Americana; Ultimo Decennio, exhibition catalogue, Museo d'Arte della Citta di Ravenna/ Edizioni Gabriele Mazotta, Ravenna, 2000.

Everett, Deborah. "Review," *NY Arts Magazine* 5, no. 3 (March 2000), p. 89.

Deep Field Painting, exhibition catalogue, The Bertha and Karl Leubsdorf Art Gallery at Hunter College, New York, 2000. Essay by Michael Brennan.

Grasso, Sebastiano. "Walter Biggs," *Corriere Della Sera*, 18 December, 1999.

Walter Biggs, exhibition catalogue, Gian Enzo Sperone/Milliventi, 1999.

Then & Now, exhibition catalogue, The Work Space, New York, 1999. Essay by Robert M. Murdock.

David D. Brody

Lives in Brooklyn, NY

Education

1989 MFA, California Institute of the Arts, Valencia

1983 Skowhegan School of Painting and Sculpture, Skowhegan, ME

1981 BA, Harvard University, Cambridge, MA

Selected Exhibitions

2002 *Young + Brash + Abstract*, Anderson Gallery, Virginia Commonwealth University, Richmond, curated by John Yau

The Tipping Point, Locks Gallery, Philadelphia, PA, curated by David Cohen

2001 Solo show, Bill Maynes Gallery, New York, NY

Group show, Gorney Bravin & Lee, New York, NY

Group show, Flipside, Brooklyn, NY

Group show, Im in Il, Brooklyn, NY

Wall Drawings, Plus Ultra, Brooklyn, NY

2000 *Between Gesture and Glyph: Paintings by David Brody and Drew Lowenstein*, Makor Center, New York, NY, curated by David Cohen

Flashlight, Flipside, Brooklyn, NY

The End, Exit Art, New York, NY

Outside and Winter Paper, Catherine Moore Fine Arts, New York, NY

Checked, Coatroom, Museum of Modern Art, New York, NY, curated by Cindy Tower

Haulin' Ass, Post Gallery, Los Angeles, CA, curated by Joe Amrhein

Pierogi 2000: Flat Files, Yerba Buena Center, San Francisco, CA, curated by Joe Amrhein

Pierogi 200 at Yard Sale, New York, NY, cheap art sale/performance with Linda Nagaoka, curated by Barbara Pollack

2000 Group show, Bennington College, Vermont, curated by Mary Lum and Anne Pibal

1999 Solo show, Revolution, Detroit, MI

Rage for Art, Pierogi 2000, Brooklyn, NY

Hard Cell, Vilma Gold Gallery, London, curated by Mary Jane Aladren/Nylon

Architecturally Abstract, Revolution New York, New York, NY

Conversation (with Ward Shelley), 4-Walls, Brooklyn, NY

Participant Ward Shelley's *Voyage Platform*, Berlin

Awards

2000 MacDowell Fellowship

1998 Yaddo Fellowship

Brooklyn Community Access TV/Rotunda Gallery Video Grant

Selected Bibliography

"From Biofreak to Organism; An Eyewitness Account," *wburg.com* 1-4 (October 2000-June 2001).

Kalm, James. "Picture This," *NY Arts* 6, no. 3 (March 2001), p.69.

"Group Show," *The New Yorker*, February 5, 2001, p.18.

Cohen, David. *Between Gesture and Glyph* (curator's essay), February 2000.

Schmerler, Sarah. "Flashlight," *TimeOut New York* 239 (April 20-27, 2000), p.62.

Fragment of a Much Larger Thing (drawing), Pierogi Press, Vol.3, Fall 1999.

Henry Brown

Lives in New York, NY

Born

1965 Washington, DC

Education

1992 MFA, Pratt Institute, NY
1989 BA, University of Maryland
1988 BA, University of Maryland

Selected Exhibitions

2002 *Young + Brash + Abstract*, Anderson Gallery, Virginia Commonwealth University, Richmond, curated by John Yau

2001 *b/t* (*between)*, New Art Center, Newton, MA; part of 2001 Boston Cyberarts Festival

2000 *Deep Field Painting*, The Bertha and Karl Leubsdorf Art Gallery at Hunter College, New York, NY curated by Michael Brennan

Awards

2002 Millay Colony for the Arts, Artist's Residency, Austerlitz, NY

1999 Yaddo Artist's Residency, Saratoga Springs, NY

Selected Bibliography

Boston Cyberarts Festival Catalogue 2001, CD-ROM catalogue, Boston Cyberarts Inc., 2001.

*b/t**, exhibition catalogue, New Art Center, 2001.

Everett, Deborah. "Deep Field Painting," *NY Arts Magazine* 5, no. 3 (March 2000).

Deep Field Painting, exhibition catalogue, The Bertha and Karl Leubsdorf Art Gallery at Hunter College, New York, 2000. Essay by Michael Brennan.

Steven Charles

Lives in Brooklyn, NY

Born

1967 Birkenhead, England

Education

1996 MFA, Temple University, Rome, Italy

1994 BFA, University of North Texas, Denton

Selected Exhibitions

2002 *Young + Brash + Abstract*, Anderson Gallery, Virginia Commonwealth University, Richmond, curated by John Yau

2001 *crclgogobaroanst*, Pierogi, Brooklyn, NY

Brooklyn!, Palm Beach Institute of Contemporary Art, Palm Beach, FL

The Hard And The Soft, Thomas Korzelius Fine Art, New York, NY

Pierogi 2000: Flat Files, Block Artspace, Kansas City Art Institute, Kansas City, MO

2000 *Haulin' Ass*, Post Gallery, Los Angeles, CA

Multiple Sensations, Yerba Buena Center for the Arts, San Francisco, CA

nowhere fast, Pierogi, Brooklyn, NY

Live from New York, Haines Gallery, San Francisco, CA, curated by Kim Wauson

1999 *In Tense*, Videoland Art Space, New York, NY, Curated by Jeff Gleich

Pierogi 2000: Flat Files, Rosenwald-Wolf Gallery, University of The Arts, Philadelphia, PA

Awards

2000 Pollock-Krasner Foundation

Selected Bibliography

Ebony, David. "David's Ebony's Top Ten," *Artnet*, June 27, 2000.

Smith, Roberta. "Steven Charles: Nowhere Fast," *The New York Times*, April 28, 2000.

Viveros-Fauné, Christian. "Fabstraction," *New York Press*, April 26–May 2, 2000.

Muro, Matt, and Sarah Douglas. "Report: Art in Billburg," *The New York Times* online: New York Today, April 4, 2000.

Douglas, Sarah. "Steven Charles: Going Nowhere Fast," *The New York Times* online: New York Today, April 7, 2000.

Bonetti, David. "Gallery Watch: Driven to dynamic abstraction," *San Francisco Examiner*, January 28, 2000.

Baker, Kenneth. "Fears, Hopes–Address Unknown," *San Francisco Chronicle*, January 22, 2000.

Theresa Chong

Lives in New York, NY

Born

1965 Seoul, Korea

Education

1991 MFA, School of Visual Arts, New York, NY

1989 BFA, Boston University

1984-85 Oberlin College, Oberlin, OH

Selected Exhibitions

2002 *Young + Brash + Abstract*, Anderson Gallery, Virginia Commonwealth University, Richmond, curated by John Yau

2001 *Theresa Chong*: Paintings, Danese, New York, NY

Finely Drawn: A Recent Gift of Contemporary Drawings, Weatherspoon Art Gallery, Greensboro, NC

Summer Group Exhibition, Danese, New York, NY

Calligraphic Legacy, Transamerica Pyramid Lobby Galleries, San Francisco, CA

The Draftsman's Colors: 14 New Acquisitions from Johns to Chong, Whitney Museum of American Art, New York, NY

2000 *ArtChicago 2000*, Festival Hall, Chicago, IL

Collecting Drawings Not Artists: Gifts from the Collection of Sarah and Werner Kramarsky, Fogg Art Museum, Harvard University, Boston, MA

1999 *Popper Etudes No. 1 & No. 2, Opus 73: Woodcut Drawings*, Danese, New York, NY

New Work: Drawings, Hosfelt, San Francisco, CA

Between Then and Now, The Work Space, New York, NY

Selected Bibliography

Johnson, Ken. "Theresa Chong," *The New York Times*, October 12, 2001.

Goodman, Jonathan. "Theresa Chong," *Art in America* 88, no. 4 (April 2000), illus.

Brennan, Michael. "Painters Journal," *artnet.com/Magazine*, October 29, 1999, illus.

Tabios, Eileen. "Theresa Chong Addresses Space in Flux," *The Asian Pacific American Journal* 7, no. 2 (Winter/Spring 1999), illus.

Christopher Francione

Lives in Philadelphia, PA

Born

1972 Devon, PA

Education

2001 MFA, Maryland Institute College of Art, Baltimore

1997 BA, The University of Delaware, Newark

Selected Exhibitions

2002 *Young + Brash + Abstract*, Anderson Gallery, Virginia Commonwealth University, Richmond, curated by John Yau

2001 *Salon 4*, Oni Gallery, Boston, MA

Spunky, Exit Art, New York, NY

Artscape, Baltimore, MD

This is Nonotech, Whole Gallery, Baltimore, MD

Thesis Exhibition, Decker Gallery, Maryland Institute College of Art, Baltimore

Do It, Meyerhoff Gallery, Maryland Institute College of Art, Baltimore

2000 *Mount Royal Group Show*, Fox Gallery, Maryland Institute College of Art, Baltimore

Group Show, Whole Gallery, Baltimore, MD

1999 *@$%#! And Giggles*, independently curated group show, Goldstar, Chicago, IL

Oddbirds Auction, Oddbirds Studio, Chicago, IL

Awards

2001 The Walters Art Gallery Travel Grant, Baltimore, MD

Kathleen Kucka

Lives in New York, NY

Born

Hartford, CT

Education

1994 MFA, Hunter College, Graduate School of Art, New York, NY

1984 BFA, The Cooper Union for the Advancement of Science and Art, New York, NY

Selected Exhibitions

2002 *Young + Brash + Abstract*, Anderson Gallery, Virginia Commonwealth University, Richmond, curated by John Yau

2001 Solo show, Jeffrey Coploff Gallery, New York, NY

That Which Remains, Bernadette Salvage Fine Art, Brooklyn, NY, curated by Mo Eich

Burn: Artists Play with Fire, The Norton Museum of Art, West Palm Beach, FL

Pierogi 2000: Flat Files, Yerba Buena Center for the Arts, San Francisco, CA; Post Gallery, Los Angeles, CA; Block Art Space, Kansas City, MI

2000 Group show, Jeffrey Coploff Fine Art Ltd., New York, NY

Fluid Flow, James Graham and Sons, New York, NY

Eye Candy: Contemporary West and East Coast Women Painters, California State University, San Bernardino/The Visual Arts Center, California State University, Fullerton

1999 Solo show, Jeffrey Coploff Gallery, New York, NY

24/7 The Inaugural Exhibition of The Nantista Discoveries Series, Guild Hall Museum, East Hampton, NY

Awards

1995 The Nancy Ashton Memorial Fund Award, Hunter College, New York.

1991 The Alternative Worksite, Bemis Foundation, Omaha, Nebraska, Artist's Residence.

Selected Bibliography

Schudel, Matt. "Fire Works," *The Sun Sentinel*, April 2001, Fort Lauderdale, FL.

Korotkin, Joyce. "Kathleen Kucka," *The New York Art World.com*, April 2001.

Burn: Artists Play with Fire, The Norton Museum of Art, West Palm Beach, FL, 2001.

Schmerler, Sarah. "Fluid Flow," *Time Out: New York*, July 27-August 3, 2000.

Knaff, Devorah. "Eye Candy by Women Reveals Beauty Beyond Good Looks," *The Press Enterprise*, April 19, 2000, Los Angeles, CA.

Johnson, Ken. "Kathleen Kucka," *The New York Times*, March 19, 1999.

Scott, Sue. "Kathleen Kucka," Review : *The Critical State of Visual Art in New York*, March 15, 1999.

OK This is So, Pierogi Press, New York, NY, 1999.

Twenty Four Seven; The Inagural Exhibition of Nantista Discoveries Series, Guild Hall of East Hampton, 1999.

Jennifer Riley

Lives in Boston, MA

Education

2000 MFA, The Milton Avery Graduate School of the Arts at Bard College, Annandale-on-Hudson, NY

1991 BFA, Tufts University, Medford, MA; The School of the Museum of Fine Arts, Boston, MA

1986 Diplome Superieur d'Eetudes Francais, Universite de Rouen, France; L'Ecole des BeauxArts, Rouen, France

Selected Exhibitions

2002 *Young + Brash + Abstract*, Anderson Gallery, Virginia Commonwealth University, Richmond, curated by John Yau

Uncommon Marriages, Chicago Arts Council, Chicago, IL, curated by Margie Vecchio

MA Solo Show, Beth Urdang Gallery, Boston, MA

2001 *A Day Without Art*, Barbara Krakow Gallery, Boston MA

150 x 150, The Gallery at Green Street, Boston, MA

The Infinite Playground, Boston Center for the Arts, Boston, MA

Color-Light-Color, Massachusetts College of Art, Boston MA, co-curated by Jennifer Riley and Taylor Davis

2000 *New York Classicism Now*, Hirschl & Adler Galleries, New York, NY

Solo show, Beth Urdang Gallery, Boston, MA

MFA Thesis Show, The Milton Avery Graduate School of the Arts at Bard College, Annandale-on-Hudson, NY

New York Area MFA, Hunter College Art Gallery, New York, NY

Selected Exhibitions *(continued)*

1999 *New Works*, Betty Wasserman Fine Art, New York, NY

Idioscapes, The Mills Gallery, Boston Center for the Arts, Boston, MA

More Abstract, MPG, Boston, MA

Awards

2000 Lee Krasner Memorial Scholarship

Selected Bibliography

Johnson, Ken. "New York Classicism Now," *The New York Times*, September 8, 2000.

Kramer, Hilton. "New York Classicism Now," *The New York Observer*, July 17, 2000.

Korotkin, Joyce. "New York Classicism Now," *The New York Art World*, September 2000. *The New Yorker*, August 14, 2000.

McQuaid, Kate. Review of solo exhibition, *The Boston Globe*, July 8, 2000.

Long, Charles, M., and Marco Zarattini. "Symphonic Chromatic Stripes," *The Beacon Hill Back Bay Chronicle*, 2000.

Temin, Christine. "Idioscapes," *The Boston Globe*, September 8, 1999.

Sherman, Mary. Review of *Idioscapes*, *The Boston Herald*, August 1999.

Lisa Stefanelli

Lives in New York City, NY

Education

1989 BFA, Rhode Island School of Design

Selected Exhibitions

2002 *Young + Brash + Abstract*, Anderson Gallery, Virginia Commonwealth University, Richmond, curated by John Yau

2001 *Skin Deep*, Islip Museum of Art, Islip, NY

Pioneering Spirit, Comite Colbert/Downtown Arts Projects, New York, NY

The Hard and The Soft, Thomas Korzelius Gallery, New York, NY

Some (Are) Painting, John Gibson Gallery, New York, NY

Specifically Painting, Edward Thorp Gallery, New York, NY

2000 Solo show, Pierogi 2000, Brooklyn, New York, NY

Abstraction in Painting Today, Castle Gallery, The College of New Rochelle, New Rochelle, NY

1999 Rosenwald-Wolf Gallery, University of the Arts, Philadelphia, PA

Road Show, DFN Gallery, New York, NY

A Room With a View, Sixth@Prince Fine Art, New York, NY

Selected Bibliography

Johnson, Ken. “Art Guide,” *The New York Times*, July 6, 2001.

Johnson, Ken. "Some (Are) Painting,” Art in Review, *The New York Times*, June 29, 2001.

Johnson, Ken. “Art Guide,” *The New York Times*, Friday February 2, 2001.

Youens, Rachel. “The Speed of Arabesque,” *Article Magazine*, www.articlemagazine.com, December 2000.

Lombardi, D. Dominick. “Abstracting the Meaning,” *The New York Times*, September 26, 2000.

Gibson, David. “Lisa Stefanelli: Pierogi 2000,” review, *Zing Magazine* 13 (November 2000).

Henry, Max. “In the Galleries,” *Flashart*, May/June 2000.

Mendelsohn, Meredith. “Weekend Update,” *Artnet*, April 5, 2000.

Article Magazine, selected portfolio, September 1999.

Hiroshi Tachibana

Lives in New York, NY

Born

1970 Hyogo, Japan

Education

2001 MFA, The Milton Avery Graduate School of the Arts at Bard College, Annandale-on-Hudson, NY

1998 BFA, School of Visual Arts, New York, NY

Selected Exhibitions

2002 *Young + Brash + Abstract*, Anderson Gallery, Virginia Commonwealth University, Richmond, curated by John Yau

2001 *An Annual Invitational Show*, Core Gallery, New Paltz, NY

MFA Thesis Exhibition, UBS Exhibition Center, Red Hook, NY

2000 *Tracking*, Artemesia Gallery, Chicago, IL

1999 Westside Gallery, New York, NY

Awards

1991 4th Prize, Hyogo Annual Juried Exhibition, Japan

Ana Vilarrasa

Lives in New York, NY

Born

1963 Madrid, Spain

Education

1989 MFA, School of Visual Arts, New York, NY

1986 BFA, Universidad Complutense de Madrid, Spain

Selected Exhibitions

2002 *Young + Brash + Abstract*, Anderson Gallery, Virginia Commonwealth University, Richmond, curated by John Yau

2000 Two-person show with Miquel Mont, Galeria Trinta, Santiago, Spain.

1999 *Recent Work on Museum Pieces*, solo exhibition, Galeria Alvarez, Porto, Portugal

1998 Robert McClain & Co., Houston, TX

Selected Bibliography

Almunia 4 (Fall-Winter 1999-2000), center insert.

Recent Work on Museum Pieces, exhibition catalogue, Galeria Alvarez, Porto, Portugal, September-November 1999.

Exhibition Checklist

Walter Biggs
Lava
1992-93
Mixed media on linen
14" x 11"
Courtesy of the artist

Walter Biggs
Red Devil
2001
Mixed media on linen
38" x 38"
Courtesy of the artist

Walter Biggs
Water Painting
1998-99
Mixed media on linen
63" x 84"
Courtesy of the artist

David Brody
Fragment of Much Larger Thing: Reticulum
2002
162" x 249" Marker or pencil on wall
Courtesy of the artist

David Brody
Region 32
1998
Acrylic on canvas on board
48" x 96"
Courtesy of the West Collection at SEI

David Brody
Region 36
2000
Acrylic on canvas on board
48" x 48"
Courtesy of the artist and
Gorney Bravin + Lee New York, NY

Henry Brown
Deviation II
2000
Acrylic, pencil, gesso on canvas
60" x 72"
Courtesy of the artist

Henry Brown
Reversal
2001
Acrylic, pencil, gesso on canvas
60" x 60"
Courtesy of the artist

Henry Brown
Interlock
2001
Acrylic, pencil, gesso on canvas
60" diameter
Courtesy of the artist

Steven Charles
eifoinbysetwin
2000
Enamel on canvas
84" x 72"
Courtesy of the artist and Pierogi,
Brooklyn, NY

Steven Charles
flefpist
2001
Enamel on canvas
40" x 36"
Courtesy of the artist and Pierogi,
Brooklyn, NY

Steven Charles
thisonme
2001
Enamel and white gold leaf on canvas
13 1/2" x 12"
Courtesy of the artist and Pierogi,
Brooklyn, NY

Theresa Chong
Untitled
2001
Oil on linen
60" x 80"
Courtesy of the artist and Danese
New York City, NY

Theresa Chong
Untitled
2001
Oil on linen
66" x 84"
Courtesy of the artist and Danese
New York City, NY

Christopher Francione
Pink
2001
Latex paint and calk on canvas
60" x 60"
Courtesy of the artist

Christopher Francione
Touchdown
2001
Latex paint and calk on canvas
60" x 60"
Courtesy of the artist

Christopher Francione
Untitled
2001
Enamel on wood panel
36" x 42"
Courtesy of the artist

Kathleen Kucka
Petite L'une au L'autre
2001
Acrylic on aluminum
22" x 22"
Courtesy of the artist

Kathleen Kucka
Grip, Grab
2000
Acrylic paint on aluminum
60" x 40"
Courtesy of the artist

Kathleen Kucka
Untitled Fall #2
2000
Acrylic paint on aluminum
60" x 40"
Courtesy of the artist

Jennifer Riley
New Rules for Romance
2000
Oil on canvas
66" x 70"
Courtesy of the artist

Jennifer Riley
Borrowed Kisses
2000
Oil on canvas
68" x 72"
Courtesy of the artist

Jennifer Riley
Biological Flutter
2001
Oil on canvas
50" x 62"
Courtesy of the artist

Lisa Stefanelli
Thornfield (The Horse Chestnut at Thornfield)
2001
Oil on canvas
81" x 65"
Courtesy of the artist

Lisa Stefanelli
Twisted Sister
2000-01
Oil on board
66" x 55"
Courtesy of the artist and Pierogi,
Brooklyn, NY

Lisa Stefanelli
The Grass Widow
2001
Oil and enamel on aluminum
24" x 36"
Courtesy of the artist and Pierogi,
Brooklyn, NY

Hiroshi Tachibana
Monster of the Room
2001
Oil and pencil on canvas
56" x 66"
Courtesy of the artist

Hiroshi Tachibana
Layer of Joke
2001
Oil and pencil on canvas
50" x 60"
Courtesy of the artist

Hiroshi Tachibana
Route 209
2001
Oil and pencil on canvas
48" x 60"
Courtesy of the artist

Ana Vilarrasa
Comic Reason 3
1999
Oil on wood
15 3/4" x 15 3/4" x 3 3/4"
Courtesy of the artist

Ana Vilarrasa
White & Purple Edge
2000
Oil on wood
18" x 18" x 5"
Courtesy of the artist

Ana Vilarrasa
Purple & White Edge
2000
Oil on wood
18" x 18" x 5"
Courtesy of the artist

Acknowledgments

Special thanks to the following individuals and organizations for their important contributions towards this exhibition and catalogue: John Yau and the artists; Laura Chessin, for her intuition, patience and insight in the design of this catalogue; George Cruger, editor; James Henderson, for transcribing the panel discussion; Patricia Lyons, exhibition photographer; Jay Paul, photographer; Maliya Rooney and the dedicated staff of Colormark for printing this publication; Howell Perkins, Virginia Museum of Fine Arts; Danese, New York, NY; Gorney Bravin + Lee, New York, NY; Pierogi, Brooklyn, NY; and the West Collection at SEI.

Thanks to the Anderson Gallery staff: Amy Moorefield; Assistant Professor, Assistant Director and Curator of Collections, Leon Roper; Assistant Professor, Gallery Manager; Shelagh Greenwood, Special Projects Coordinator. Special thanks to Pat Soden, Director, and the staff of the University of Washington Press.